MEMORIES

OF A

TEACHING

LIFE

IN

MUSIC

The Autobiography

of Wachtang Botso Korisheli

ISBN: 978-0-557-55732-5

TABLE OF CONTENTS

INTRODUCTION

I have been encouraged and asked over and over to put down my experiences. I have finally decided to introduce my life to my students, friends and family, to pick some episodes to help them to understand a person's faith when one loses everything, literally everything, and yet does not give up having faith in humanity.

In addition, I have decided to explain the conditions and the history of my country, Georgia. The idea was first suggested to me by my English professor and dear friend, Prof. Marvin Mudrick. He often heard me complaining how few people knew where Georgia was, and who Georgians were. Most of my acquaintances would associate Georgia with the state of Georgia in America. "Why don't you write a term paper? I'll print it for you, and if someone questions, hand it to him." The term paper which I wrote for him as a student at UCSB, "The Struggle of the Caucasian People for Independence," can be found in the Appendix , and I hope it will enlighten all my friends and students.

To describe the conditions during the spread of communism in the Soviet Union I have occasionally used

1

fictional names, although the stories and happenings were experienced and told by my grandparents. All the stages of my life which resembles a tumbleweed are written in close chronological order, and if my students gain some advice to follow my footsteps, I will be a very well-rewarded man.

Within the episodes and experiences I am trying to convey the importance of steps I took and found helpful to teach others. They are:

1. Do not contradict or try to change the nature of Nature — I mean the elements of our existence: air, water, animals, and earth.

2. Skill and imitation are part of learning, but you must grow out of imitation to create your own identity.

3. It is important to learn the demands of your body and system, your intuitions, to stay well-adjusted to the demands of our existence.

These points are woven in my stories and the reader will find them in different situations.

In discussing my plan to write my autobiography, my son, my colleagues, and my students encouraged me to write just the way I talk and not standardize my

English. I have tried to follow their advice, and my hope is that you will enjoy as much as they have.

Special thanks to my best friend, Dick Rush, my son Temmo, and my wife Margaret for their assistance and loving support throughout this project. My special thanks to my student and friend, Joan Pedersen, for her assistance in completing this work.

And finally, I dedicate my work to my students, parents and family, who taught me so much and shaped my life and personality.

PROLOGUE

There will be peace in our world
if we follow what Paul Celan said,
"I am most I when I am you."

The streetcar we had to take early, very early, was almost empty. By the time we reached the outskirts of the city limits, it was just my mother and me and the streetcar conductor. The end station was the place where the streetcar had to turn around, be checked and go back to town. That end station was where the political prison was located. My father had been taken there a few days before.

We were earlier than what our designated time was to see Father. We slowly approached the iron gate. The officer at the gate asked for the papers. He was not friendly and looked very official.

After he read the permit, I saw his face go softer.

"You are too early for the visitation."

We did not answer. I felt that he was trying to be nicer. Did he know my father?

He must have, because he opened the gate and said, "Come in anyway. Go through that door on the left and wait there. That is the visiting room. Someone will bring your father in." He looked at me the whole time.

The room was cold. There was nothing in it except a long wooden bench on the opposite wall behind two lines of iron bars, separated about two feet, which ran across the width of the room. The door opened behind the iron bars and my father entered with another officer. I did not know that I was seeing my dad for the last time, and I hurried to grab his hand. The officer stopped me quickly to check our hands, palms up.

"OK," he called and I held one hand and Mother the other.

Father talked to me most of the time. Listening to his voice I loved so much, I felt there was something different about his tone and the weight of his speech. He usually talked in slow, short sentences with lots of pauses in between. He always had a sedentary pace. I think he was giving me time to get the meaning and essence of what he was telling me.

This time he seemed to hurry to tell me more, talked faster. First I considered the twenty minutes we were allowed to see him, then a heart-sinking thought struck me: is he going to be sent to Siberia? Will I see him again? I was getting panicky. Time was running out. He squeezed my hand again and I started walking backwards toward the door. I saw him waving, and I stumbled on something. It may have been my own foot. I almost fell.

I heard Dad's voice like before. "Are you all right?"

"Yes, I am, Dad."

"Remember, I will be with you all the time."

These last words never left me.

We got in the same streetcar which was turned around and ready to go back to town. No one was in the car except my mother and myself and the conductor who came to check our tickets. I was crying silently, and my tears were running down my face. I did not have any desire to wipe my eyes.

The conductor stopped, looked at me for a long time. I was holding Mom's hand who was also crying. The conductor put his hand on my shoulder and squeezed affectionately.

It felt like my father's hand. I remembered all Dad's aphorisms. "Whoever and wherever, if you are in trouble, put your hand on my shoulder and I'll walk with you." And then his last call, "Remember, I will be with you all the time."

The warm hand of our conductor on my shoulder gave me feelings which stayed with me the rest of my life. All teachers and friends I have met have replaced my parents. I developed the insight that my Mom and Dad were talking through them. I have never met an evil person, and I know I never will.

CHAPTER ONE:

BEGINNINGS

When one loses everything,
there is one thing one can keep:
hope.

I was fifteen years old when my father was taken away from us.

"ACTOR PLATON KORISHELI ACCUSED OF UNDERMINING SOVIET SYSTEM" blared the newspaper headlines. Father and Mother were greatly respected and loved by Georgians and they were famous throughout the country. We waited and waited for Dad to come home that evening, and then in the morning I had to go to school.

Another day passed without Father, and Mother could not wait any more.

"You go to school," she told me, and I knew that she was going to the government building to find out the details. The school turned out to be estranged from me. The students were cautious to talk to me, except my close friends. The teachers were reserved to comfort me, although I felt that they were trying to express some sympathy. Their expressions were telling me that they were sharing my sorrows.

I was confused and lost, but my close friends whispered to me that the teachers had announced in their classrooms, "Botso's father was imprisoned as an enemy of the Soviet Union."

There was another official statement in the morning newspaper. I went to the school principal and asked if I could be excused to go home to see my mother.

"Of course you can. Do you have money for the streetcar?"

I usually walked home and it was nice of him to offer some help.

"Yes, I do. Thank you very much."

He stood by the door watching me until my streetcar came. I waved at him and got a two-arm wave back from him.

Mother was home and we hugged each other for a long time. The next day, I went to the department of the KGB and asked the officer at the door if I could see someone who would let me see my father, who had been taken away.

"Wait here."

He went to the next room. When he came back, he asked me to follow him. We went into a small room with one desk on each side, with an officer sitting at one of them.

He waited till we were alone, and then said, "Sit down."

I sat in the other chair. He was silent for a while and I was worried.

"You love your dad?"

"Yes, sir." He was silent again.

Then, "I'll allow you and your mother to see your dad tomorrow at the political prison for twenty minutes."

He gave me the address and a permission slip.

We got up early the next day and caught the streetcar to take us to the end of town where the prison was. We were earlier than the specified time, but the guard let us in the waiting room, with two rows of iron bars an arm's length apart dividing the room.

Father came in with another officer and asked if he could hold our hands. The men wanted to see all six open palms, which we did.

"Yes, you may," the officer said somewhat respectfully.

Father talked to me most of the twenty minutes and held mother's hands. Since that day, I have lived seventy years, but I still know every word he passed to me. I catch myself repeating and reciting the conversation, trying to imitate his warm voice I loved so much.

"Do not go to sleep without asking yourself, did I do enough work for the day?"

"Do not depend on rumors. Always listen to the other side."

"Listen more, and talk less."

"The songs you played for me sounded warm, and always telling me something. Never lose that."

"Remember on our hikes, you thought you would not make it over the steep mountain? You always did make it because you wanted to. Never give up!"

"Do not leave things unfinished. You start; make sure you finish."

"Remember that only through your patience you can survive the troubles and problems."

"Do not repeat second-hand news. Find the truth."

"Always make sure that your friends and relatives feel at home in your home."

"If you are upset or depressed, do some hard physical work."

He told me stories and examples for all this advice while holding Mom's hand. Mom was silent, but I could feel that she was controlling her tears. The officer let us talk longer than twenty minutes. I sensed that he respected my father.

At that time, I did not know that I was seeing him for the last time.

Later, the official charge read: "Platon Korisheli, under Sandro Akhmeteli's leadership, was active in counterrevolution. Korisheli did not feel that he had engaged in an act of sedition, but did confess that he was in sympathy with Akhmeteli's idea of an independent Caucasia."

According to reports, my father was accused of collaborating with Akhmeteli, the theatre director; he told the prosecutor that he did not feel guilty, but if the system thought that he was, they should do what they had to do. The verdict was announced: "Execution."

When I went back to school, I could not help but feel that the students and the teachers were trying to avoid me.

Then it happened: a popular senior by the name of Niko, who walked tall and wore the uniform of the Komsomol (young candidates for the Communist Party), approached me during the long recess. I was surrounded by my close friends who never left me and were always on my side.

"Botso! I have a great suggestion for you!" My friends froze for a moment. I think they imagined what was going to happen, and it did. "Botso! In three days we have a big school assembly, and I would like to help you to join the Komsomol organization. I'll call you on the stage and all you have to do is denounce your father in public—" He could not finish the sentence. My friends came closer to me, to comfort me. They saw that I was shaking and boiling.

I do not know where I got the power. Niko was taller and stronger than I was. I charged with all my being and all my soul. I threw him down and started beating him very brutally. We were pulled apart by my friends. He was bleeding all over his face. Several teachers ran over, including the principal, who took me to his office and instructed me to go home and to bring my mother the next day.

After my Mom's meeting with the principal, I was surprised when they allowed me to resume my studies, under the condition that I apologize to Niko. My friends told me that the teachers did not put the blame on me. I returned to school, but I never did apologize to Niko.

What happened to me the third day opened the road towards my future.

Our mathematics professor, W. Abdusheli, was highly respected and admired in all educational fields. He rarely associated with anyone at school. His students revered and respected him beyond limits. No one had ever seen Prof. Abdusheli talking to a student outside the classroom.

On that day, after the math lesson, during the long recess, Prof. Abdusheli picked up his books and motioned me to his side.

"Your dad is a very good man," he said, putting his arm around my shoulder. We walked through the hallway. Students and teachers made room for us, looking astounded. It was an unusual sight for the school.

"Your father is right; the stage should be for the people and society, and not for the ruling party," he continued. I was catching surprised looks from students and teachers and felt like I was floating in heaven.

How did he know my father's favorite statement? He continued the conversation for the entire twenty minutes of recess. I still think that he was taking my Dad's place and making sure that I would not get depressed and develop some inferiority complexes. He was trying to make me proud.

I did not only feel happy and proud, but I also became a great math student, and I developed into a mature thinker. Prof. Abdusheli was sharing my father's ideas. He lit a torch for the rest of my life.

School life was going fine, but other hard times were ahead.

Our home was confiscated by the KGB. Three of the four rooms downstairs were sealed with strings and red wax seals with the sign of the hammer and sickle. The second story was reserved for a party member's family. Mother and I were given one room (which had been my parents' bedroom), with access to the kitchen and bathroom.

I could not get rid of the urge to cut the string and go into my own room, or to see my dad's library again. Mom started buying and collecting warm clothing in a large suitcase, thinking of Siberia. That was a common practice, sending the wives of political prisoners to Siberia.

I hated that suitcase. I could not sleep very well, thinking of losing Mom also.

After one month, our life changed again. One night after 2 a.m., my dog Omar started to bark and would not stop. I went to the gate, and there were two officers with a lady and two small children in a big black car. First I was scared, thinking they have come to get Mom. We had heard that it was a common practice to make arrests after midnight in order not to arouse the neighbors' curiosity. I put my dog in our room. I must have looked very scared.

"Do not worry. We are going to unseal one room, and this family is going to live here for a while."

I took them to the sealed rooms. They already knew which one to open. It was my father's library.

"How old are you?"

"Fifteen," I said.

They whispered together a while.

"When will you be sixteen?"

"This coming Christmas."

"Well, you can be a witness and sign this paper. It just proves that we brought the family to your house, room number one."

After cutting the string and opening the door, they asked me to show the things inside. The woman used my father's sofa to put down the children. I signed the paper, and the officers left. My mom came out. She looked very disturbed. I think she also thought that they had come for her.

We offered some help to accommodate the family. The Pataridzes turned out to be very beautiful people and we soon became good friends. Having the same fate brought us even closer.

Soon I felt responsible for all these ladies. I wanted to be their protector. I started doing chores for them. I would go shopping for all of us and my dog started to love them. I was worried they might be bothered by my piano practicing because my piano could be heard all over the house, but they liked it. I felt important and needed. It was a good feeling.

A week later, Omar started an alarming barking again. It was after 2 a.m. I had to perform the same duties again. Two officers brought another family: a mother, daughter and elderly grandmother. I signed the paper; they opened the next room (my old bedroom). The officers had no questions, only a short comment: "You have a vicious dog."

This time, it was my room that got occupied. I was very attached to everything in it, but somehow I felt satisfied because the family, the Gvishianis, were so helpless and dependent on us. I was becoming a full-fledged housekeeper.

Mother was asked to resign from the Rustaveli Theatre. She accepted an invitation to join a traveling performing troupe, so that we could keep our household together.

Two days later, the same two men from the KGB showed up. This time, I kept Omar locked up. I think he was waking up the neighbors.

I was expecting the last empty room to be occupied. That was the largest, the dining room. But the officers told me the room was too large for a single lady. I looked behind them and there were no children. The lady had a large suitcase, similar to the one Mom kept ready.

She looked scared and kept very quiet. The officers told me that they would be sending a carpenter to divide the room because there was more than one family to be placed there.

We all felt as one family and often shared our fears. All of our families' fathers were sent to Siberia, except the last single lady's husband was executed as we were told. I was hoping they would not come again because our rooms were occupied, but I was wrong. This time they drove the car to the gate at 1 p.m. After I opened the gate, four men came in. My heart started beating so hard that it felt like it would jump out of my chest. They asked for room three. That was the single lady's room. There were no papers to sign. They asked me to go back to my room. In my room, mom and I heard the single lady crying. I peeked out and saw the four men taking her and her suitcase to the car. The answer was simple: Siberia. That was the usual procedure. I found myself developing a strong sense of responsibility for the orphan families and for my mom, so I approached Mom with a suggestion to unlock her suitcase. I needed to find some work to help her income. That suitcase was always an eye-sore for me. "What will you do? You are busy with your schoolwork and practice," she said.

"My Saturday's are available and I would very much like to find a studio job — a dancing studio. I know some friends who were taking dancing lessons and they need an accompanist on the piano."

All I needed to do was learn a few songs. I already knew some of the dancing tunes. And I also knew that most choreographers knew my family and they would be most cooperative. So, after visiting a couple studios, I got the job. All I had to give up was my favorite sport, soccer. After school, coming home, I would always grab a slice of bread and cheese and go out on the street. Some dozen boys divided into two teams — two stones on each side for the goal posts and the game was on. I had to give that time up for homework and practice. We were lucky to keep our piano in our room, and I was able to practice while Mom was at work. I tried not to interrupt her memorization exercises for the plays. I have the most pleasant memories of practicing the piano.

The boys were not playing soccer games at that time, and I discovered something wonderful. After I finished my scales and exercises and etudes and assigned pieces, I loved to improvise melodies, and I noticed that a window across the street would open up and a young beautiful lady, Miriam was her name, would sit on the frame of the window and put her head on the frame, close her eyes and listen to me. Mother did not have to remind me to practice anymore. Miriam's listening helped my expressiveness in phrases and in my improvisation. It became my habit for all my life.

Almost three months went by and the third room was still sealed and empty. We were all hoping that the troubles were over, but again at 2 a.m. my dog Omar started the same alarming bark, as if he knew what was going to happen. This time a family with two very young children was put in room three. I was hoping they would not be disturbed by my practicing. The piano was on a wall against their room. We were very lucky again. The family was wonderful and the mother was more than pleased to hear my music and practicing. My studies were going well.

There were two more teachers who paved my future. Professor Vardiashvili was our world literature teacher. She knew my family's suffering and the situation we were in. She approached me with an idea to write a term paper about my feelings for music. I worked very eagerly on that project and she was very pleased. She read the paper to the class and later gave me wonderful advice about writing essays. Finally she asked me to write a short play, a skit, and since the class was enthused about it, we performed it in the classroom. She became instrumental for my future writings.

Mom insisted that I learn a foreign language. French was usually the popular language, but I was attached to German. There's a special story about this attachment. In school we had had a foreign language teacher for one year in German. Frau Meiers was very strict. Very unfriendly. And the class was suffering. She would come into the room like a good old sergeant and we would all have to stand up in unison and she would command us to sit down in a very commanding tone. In German, she would say, "Hinsetzen!" (Sit down!) Next she would take out the class roster and read the names. You had to stand up straight and answer loudly in German, "Anwesend" and that meant that you were there. "Ich bin anwesend" — "I am here." Now, my friend Andro and I used to hike sometimes behind our house. Up in the hills was a small creek running down the hill. There were lots of cute little frogs that we used to catch and play with. Andro said, "Let's collect them." When the frogs sat in darkness and then you exposed them to the light, they had a tendency to jump. We noticed that when we collected them and put them in the box, they did exactly the same thing — we opened the box and they jumped. So our idea was that when Frau Meiers came to the classroom in first period, we would put the class roster in the box with the frogs and when she opened it, the frogs would jump at her and maybe that would scare her to stay away from us.

"Let's catch some frogs," said Andro. And we did.

She had the first period, as I said, and we went to the custodian and told him we had some extra work to do and asked if he would let us in earlier. He was glad to do it for us and we put our roster in the drawer and then the frogs. There were about 15 of them. We told the class what we were doing and when she came in, we stood up like one man — all together — very impressive and straight in attention. "Hinsetzen!" she commanded. Everyone's heart was beating loud. She opened the drawer and here is what happened. The good frogs jumped at her breast. She fell over with her chair and fainted. An alarm was given, nurses came and revived her. The class was locked in and no one could get out. Frau Meiers was taken out on a stretcher. The principal, vice principal and the custodian (who had difficulty catching all 15 of them) finally caught all the frogs and took them out.

"Now, you all know what you did," the principal said. "I want to know who is responsible for this treacherous deed. Stand up."

There was a little pause and silence. Andro and I were ready to get up, but we looked around and the entire class stood up together. It was a tense and dynamic atmosphere for a while. The principal did not say anything. We stood quietly. The teachers and principal went out, and we waited five minutes until the principal came back. The bell rang and we stayed seated. The next period bell rang and we were still in the classroom. And then the door opened, and the principal came back in again. We all stood up.

"Sit down please." He took the chair himself, so we all did this together. Silence. "OK, we will have to have a conference with your parents and let you know what we are going to do. Go to your next classes and I will be in touch."

We were very surprised to find out that she left school and our punishment was postponed and never took place. We got another German teacher, and we fell in love with her. She was a delight. She was great, and we started to learn the language beautifully. The semester was over, and I told my mom that I would love to learn the German language instead of French. And I told her about Frau Schultz, our favorite teacher. Mom contacted her and I had private lessons with her every Saturday. She turned out to be a very inspiring teacher and I was eager to learn. I managed to learn the language in two years well enough to communicate very well.

"Just think, if you ever go to Germany or talk to German people, you will feel right at home. They will be surprised," she used to tell me.

My senior year came full of problems. Stalin issued a proclamation that said all sons and daughters of political enemies of the country would be subject to certain new restrictions. First, we would not be able to pursue higher education. Second, we would not be able to hold state or highly important jobs or hold a position in a responsible institution. Third, we could not become a full-fledged army recruit for the country. Mother and I discussed the problem of my future. I don't know how she came up with the solution. Perhaps she used her reputation or pressured some authorities. Or maybe my brother Leo had something to do with my placement in the working unit. I received the order to depart and be drafted in a working battalion.

Mom was asked to join the travelling theater. She was often asked to recite or read the stories to the soldiers. She was a great storyteller as I know so well. She was always in popular demand. Having Mom working, I had to take care of myself. My brother Leo, who was much older than I took care of me. After his work hours he would stop by our home and spend some time with me.

The weekends were my favorite times. Leo was in the military academy and had an officer's rank. On Sundays when Mom as not home, he used to take me to the Officers' Club. There were lots of sports and also a recreational center where Leo used to play billiards. I found out that he was an unbeatable billiard master. It was fun watching him play. I loved watching his face and eyes calculating the proper angles and strokes, always with successful results. I told him that I read W. A. Mozart's biography and he was also acclaimed as a superior pool player. Leo joked, "Well, it takes two of us to make one Mozart. You, the musician, and me, the pool master."

The day of my departure came and Mom went with me to the railroad station. She kept telling me that she was sure she would not be arrested. She knew this, she said, because the officials had told her so. She told me that I would be far from her and that I would be very near the borders of other countries. She was convinced that we would see each other again.

"Look," she said. "I'm not crying, so you do not worry." She really was not crying.

I was choking. The world did not mean anything to me.

The train started. I was hanging out of the window to see her. Mother was waving and running to keep up with the slow pace of the train. I noticed that she was not holding her body straight as she always did. Then I think I saw her collapse. I tried to run to the door and jump out. I felt arms around my shoulders. A warm hug of my comrade stopped me. I broke down and cried. Mother was right. We were put near the Polish border digging trenches in anticipation of the German invasion. We did get some Russian uniforms but no weapons.

We were put in a small group of workers with picks and shovels to dig the foxholes near the Polish border by the river Dnieper. We could feel the anxiety and fear among us. At night we knew that Germans were across the river. The sounds of rolling tanks were not

Russians. A young soldier with a rifle was supervising us and keeping us together.

The older man next to me was Armen from Armenia. We, being from neighboring countries, were stuck together. I felt safe with him. Before the dawn, he whispered to me, "Let us cross the bridge and escape." And here is what he did. There was some loose dirt near our young guard, who was taking his break and rolling tobacco in newspaper, as usual. Armen got close to him, and with a powerful swing of his shovel threw a full load of fine dirt in the guard's face. Poor soldier fell off the stump he was sitting on, and we ran to the other side of the bridge, jumped down on the other side and crawled under. In the morning we could hear a tank coming to the bridge. It stopped, and soon we could hear footsteps. We waited breathlessly for hours. The tank was silent, but we could hear soldiers' steps going back and forth. It was almost midday, and I whispered to Armen that I spoke German and I would put my handkerchief on a stick and go up. He said I should be careful and move very slowly with my hands up above my shoulders.

I crawled out and saw a young German soldier with a machine gun. As soon as he saw me he grabbed his gun and pointed it at me.

"Bitte nicht schiessen!" (Please do not shoot!) I shouted.

He kept pointing his gun at me.

"Ich bin kein Soldat." (I am not a soldier.)

He seemed puzzled.

"Bist du ein Russe?" (Are you Russian?)

"Nein. Ich bin ein Georgier." (No, I am Georgian.)

Then he wanted to know how it was that I spoke German. After a little explanation, he lowered his machine gun, and I told him that I had another friend with me who was hiding under the bridge. He told me to call him. After Armen came up with his hands way up high, the soldier lowered his gun and told us to march back where several tanks were lined up. We were told to march back where some other prisoners were gathered in a group. Armen and I were put in a prison camp. When the Germans found out my command of their language, they put me to work as a translator. My teacher had been right: the German language saved my life.

CHAPTER TWO:

THE WAR

There is one advantage to being a tumbleweed:

you'll see lots of places

After we got to the prison camp it got more crowded day by day. The Germans decided to split their prisoners in several echelons and move toward different locations in Poland. In our group, when they lined us up, we were more than 500 men. Every 50 persons was accompanied by one soldier with a machine gun, and about every 5–10 miles he would be replaced by another soldier who was dropped off by army transport trucks. The only nourishment we could gather along the road was thrown by the local farmers watching us march and feeling sorry for us. They would throw anything they had for us to catch. The guarding soldiers did not mind this help. They would even stop us to pick up the food and after it was inhaled, we marched on.

The act of diving for food reminded me of my grandma's village that had a bunch of chickens. When she was feeding them and throwing the food on the ground, the chickens would fight and grab each other's food away and run around. It looked just like that. Once, I was fortunate to catch a half a loaf of old bread. I immediately divided it into three parts — one part for the fellows on either side of me, which gave me two bodyguards, and I could devour my part of the food without being attacked. I was amazed how much energy it gave me to march on.

Our guards noticed that some could not walk very well and were getting tired. Thank God they started to give us periodic rests. Finally we reached a large fenced area — some farm storage space — and we were given warm soup. It did not matter what was in it. It felt good and it was warm.

They made a huge prison camp out of that place later. We could lie down and sleep, sleep, sleep. The nights were colder, but luckily it was summer. Sometimes we would change our positions on the ground. The outside person would get in the middle, to keep a little bit warmer when the night was cold. The camp was growing every day. The fences were extending and guards multiplying.

The camp we stayed in was not far from the city of Krakow, as I found out later. After about seven weeks the Germans who patrolled the camp and distributed the food noticed that I was asking questions in German. One day they lined us up. I sensed that something special was going to happen, and it did. A highly-decorated officer was examining people. When he came to our row, the soldiers pointed at me, telling him that I spoke German. The officer's name was Baron von Kutschenbach, a very interestingly decorated man to look at with a well-fitting uniform, shiny boots and fascinating monocle which hung on a golden chain. He put it on his right eye and then dropped it skillfully by wincing his eye socket. It almost hypnotized me. He came close to me, put up his monocle in his eye and then moved his eyebrow and nose.

"Do you speak German?"

"Yes, sir."

"How long have you been in the army?"

"I'm not in the army, sir. I am not a soldier. I am a trench digger."

He seemed to be a little confused and curious.

"You have the uniform on, don't you?"

"Yes, sir, but no weapons. Just a shovel and a pick."

"Are you Russian?"

"No, I am Georgian."

He dropped his monocle. I noticed his expression changed quickly. He motioned to his soldier (it looked like a sergeant) and gave him some orders I could not hear. That evening I was taken by the same sergeant out of the camp into a large adjacent building which looked like a storage building for a farm. The guard stopped us and wanted to know what was going on. He was shown the orders and we went on. I was taken into a large room. At a long wooden table sat high-ranking German officers. In the middle was Baron von Kutschenbach. He had his monocle in his eye and it stayed there all the time. As far as I could guess, he was the highest ranking among the others. They did not ask me to sit down, and I did not expect it. An empty chair with a nice looking cushion was right next to me. If they did ask me to sit, I would probably politely refuse because of my dirty outfit. We Georgians have that unnecessary pride sometimes.

"I told my colleagues about you speaking German quite well. We want to know how you learned it," the Baron asked. I told him about Mom's request and my private teacher's name. I also told him that my father was condemned by the Russians. There was a little pause which scared me at first.

"I want you to know that while your country had political intervention in 1918, my uncle lived there for several years and married a Georgian princess, who was a great lady, and I learned a lot about your people."

Another officer asked, "Stalin was Georgian also. What would you do if you saw him now?"

I caught my breath. "I would put him in this prison camp," I said.

That broke the ice, and they laughed and their faces were human instead of official. They started to converse for a while. I could not hear what the discussion was about and it was too fast to follow.

"How many Georgians are in the camp?" the Baron asked.

"There are five us," I said. "There could be more, but I don't think so. We usually find each other."

"Go back to camp, and in a few days we will take all five of you out of there to organize a communication group. We want you to be our translator when we talk to some captured Russian officers."

In five days, we were taken out of the prison camp and were put in a small house with three rooms. One room was for the sergeant (the same one who stood by the Baron in the camp). The middle room was for messengers and business, and the third room was for us. There was only one bed, but our sergeant brought lots of hay, and that was a luxury for us. We decided to take turns sleeping in the bed, and that worked fine. The food was coming from the regular army kitchen, and it was great. We started to function like humans again. One day the soldier brought lots of old soldiers' clothing and we were told to throw away the old dirty clothing. We still looked very funny, but we knew that we were going to stay alive. Some of my friends were still afraid that they would torture us for information, but we did not have any information whatsoever. Now we had some old German clothing, so we were going to stay alive. We never saw Baron von Kutschenbach again in Poland. Another officer kept coming out and checking on us periodically.

After six weeks we were getting closer to our German sergeant. He told us stories about Georgians which he had heard from Baron von Kutschenbach.

He said, "The Baron told us that Georgians like singing and music."

"That is a very strong tradition in our country. We sing when we work. We sing when we're having parties and many other activities," we said.

"Sing some for me." We did, and did not sound bad, I thought. "I am a musician," he said. "Next week a very important officer is going to come from Germany to see and talk to you all. I am going to surprise him with a little song I wrote for you. He is a well-known musician also, and we will have some fun."

I did not want to let him know about my musical background. He started to teach us the song. I thought it was a joke, but I didn't say anything. He asked me to teach my friends the German text for a song which was "Wir sind die Ziegen" which means "We are the goats." And then the song went something like this: "Wir sind die Ziegen nah, nah, nah, nah. Nah, nah, nah, nah." I had the suspicion that he was going to entertain his boss by making us look like goats. Actually, we may have resembled them with our ungroomed hair and beards and mustache, plus our funny uniforms — some too large and some too small. I told him we were practicing and would be ready for the show for this officer. I put the song in three-part harmony and to my surprise one Georgian, Archil was his name, had a wonderful high voice. After I got this three-part going very well, he surprised me by taking off with an impressive improvised descant, in Georgian we call it "krimanchuli." Similar to Swiss yodeling, it makes a song very lively. The song started to sound very sophisticated and beautiful. The tune was creating a very unusual four-part harmony all of the sudden with some daring, well-justified dissonances. I felt good about our surprise, and here is what happened.

The officer came, and he seemed very quiet. He had a meditative face. He asked me to translate a message from Baron von Kutschenbach to our group.

He said, "We have a certain plan for your group, and hopefully after the conference with the camp director I will tell you what we are going to do, but now my sergeant tells me that you have prepared a simple song to greet me."

The sergeant came and started introducing us. I had an uncomfortable feeling that he was trying to amuse the officer by making us subhumans. The fascist, hubristic teaching was that there were subhumans and superhumans. So we were subhumans and the German race was super-human. (In German, they would say Untermenschen und Obermenschen.) So, us looking like goats represented the subhuman by imitating animals. We sang the song beautifully for our officer. After we finished, the sergeant was looking at the officer with a very wide grin, expecting a laugh from his boss. Oh my, what happened! This was a scary situation. The officer got up slowly with a stern face and a commanding voice and turned to the sergeant.

"Did you tell me that you composed the song?"

"Yes, sir." The sergeant's face changed very abruptly.

"Did you write all these harmonies?"

"No, sir, but…"

"But what?" and then in a louder voice, "Do you know what you just heard?"

I was putting two and two together. The officer was an accomplished musician, according to the sergeant.

"Do you know the four-part harmony with the improvised obbligato *ad libitum*? Do you know the sophistication of the polyphony?"

I think he did not agree with the sergeant's fascist approach to us. He turned to us and asked me to interpret to my people.

"Tell your friends that the song you performed is very complex and beautiful and you should be proud. I'm familiar with the beautiful Georgian multi-part singing and the tradition, and I am glad I had a live performance in front of me. Are any of you musicians?"

I slowly stepped out.

"Yes, sir, I am."

I looked at the sergeant who was standing at attention, straight as a post. I kind of felt sorry for him.

We never saw our sergeant again.

The next day we were put in a low-flying transport vehicle and flown to Germany. We were placed in a small suburb town near Berlin. It was an old millhouse converted to a grain storage place. We were placed in the second story which was warm and had enough wooden bunks for us to sleep. They gave us some factory workers' outfits. We were able to shave and shower and started to look like normal people. The German who was looking after us was a nice old man and was very good to us. We had a weekly visit from Army medics to check our health. And the food was great.

About two weeks after our arrival we had a surprise visitor. Germany did not have too many Georgian immigrants. The few who were there had a good reputation in their work. Our visitor was a Georgian immigrant, Mr. Metreveli, a scholar and a great collector of unpublished folklore, stories and writings by Georgian people. He owned a little Georgian printing shop in Berlin, publishing some lost Georgian folk literature. Obtaining permission to take us out for an excursion to Berlin for a day, he showed us his printing shop and asked if we would be interested in singing on the radio. All this attention was puzzling me and I asked Mr. Metreveli about it.

"There are many more groups like yours around Berlin," he said. "I think you'll find out what the Germans are planning for you."

We took the streetcar to the radio station. It was a large, very well-equipped place. The waiting room had a beautiful grand piano. Mr. Metreveli told us to sit down and we would have to wait for a little while. He noticed that I was edging toward the piano.

"Do you play?"

"Yes, I was a music student majoring in piano."

He got excited.

"Go ahead. Play," he urged me.

My fingertips started to itch. My teacher used to tell me that if you practice properly, fingertips have the memory, and they will not let you down. I had had trouble believing that, but since that day, I do. I slowly sat down, put my fingers on the keyboard and played my favorite Chopin waltz in C-sharp minor, which I memorized for performances. The keys felt good under my fingers and I was happy. As I was playing my piece, the recording windows along the wall opened up one by one, and the technicians were looking out the window and stuck their heads out to listen. Mr. Metreveli looked at them very proudly as if to say, "Look. Georgians are not subhumans."

After we found out about similar groups staying around us, we were gathered together and sent to German army training camp in Bavaria. The camp was called Lutensee by a little town called Mittenwald. This town was famous for violin-making in Europe. They organized five companies of Georgians, about 100 in each, with German commanders. The war exercises were in the high Alps and we were instructed that the purpose of the project was to cross the Georgian Caucasian high mountains to free the country from Russians. We were outfitted in German uniforms, and the captain was a well-trained mountaineer, a great hiker and good leader. After each mountain maneuver, on the way to camp just before we entered the city of Mittenwald, he would stop us, clean and shape us up, and then would ask us to sing to the streets. That was quite an experience. We must have sounded good because all the windows would open, and people came out to the streets to watch and hear us. Our captain looked so happy and proud, and we were more than happy to help do our best to impress the captain and the population — particularly the girls!

We had a good repertoire: two Georgian songs and two German songs which the captain taught us. I practiced the German songs a lot with my people and we did sound quite good. The two Georgian songs were a shepherd song about nature, dogs and flowers, and the other one about King Vakhtang who heard bells from the sky — from heaven — and helped all the men and freed the country from invaders. The first German song was a mountain song about a flower called "Ericka," and the second was a song about a boy with black-brown hair and his girl with hair of the same color. It was unison and strong-sounding.

The good times did not last very long. We were sent north of the Caucasian mountains, a place called Nalchik. There we had to wait for Stalingrad to fall in German hands. News came that the German army was surrounded by Soviet forces, and that became the turning point of the Second World War. Germans started to retreat, and we were sent to the Crimean peninsula, which was deserted by Russians. There we had to wait for Germans to regain the eastern front of Russia. We stayed in Crimea for two and a half months, and I was attached to the headquarters in case of a need for translations.

My friend, a Georgian by the name of Tariel, and I were asked to find some place to stay with farmers. We asked around and were sent to the caretaker of a deserted rose plantation. He was a kind old man with a wooden leg. He lived alone in a small house, and we got a small room with wooden beds. To wash ourselves, we had to get the water from the well and wash outdoors, pouring the cold bucket of water over our hands and heads. We had no problem with privacy, no one lived around nearby. The rose plantation was very large, and he used to supply the Russians with rose oil for the production of perfumes. They used to export oil also. Our host always tried to be kind and helpful to accommodate us. Once, while we were washing and shaving ourselves, he came out with a gallon can of liquid and told us to use it as after-shave lotion. He put it in our curved palms and we put it on our faces, under our arms and on our necks. It smelled good. He told us that the Russians had left in such a hurry that he was stuck with five gallons of rose oil.

"This rose oil, I want you to take a couple gallons as a gift from me," he offered to us. How could we know? Here's what happened. We got dressed and went to headquarters. We were ordered to go back and wash off the strange smell that we carried. We tried, but it was impossible. We found out that one drop of the rose oil can make an entire expensive bottle of perfume. For two weeks, we tried to get rid of the smell out of our skin and hands. Nothing helped. Every day we were ordered to report and then get lost immediately. Getting lost was not easy at all. Everywhere in the village, people and soldiers knew where we were and where we stayed. We started to hate our sleeping room. If we had to be found for an emergency, all they had to do was follow the smell. Our headquarter officials were getting a little worried, and rightly so. We received orders to evacuate the Crimea. The Russians captured the city of Kiev and cut off the peninsula. The only way for us to get to the west was evacuation by sea. When we had to say good-bye to our host, he offered two gallons of the oil for each one of us to take as a gift.

"Put them in your knapsack. They are not too heavy."

"Oh, no! Thank you very much!"

It happened that two years later, when I was visiting some Georgian immigrants in Paris and was telling them the story of Crimea and the story of the rose oil and the caretaker's offer, they were aghast. They were in a panic and one of them said, "Do you realize what you did? Two gallons of rose oil would have made a millionaire out of you!" It was hard to digest for them. One little bottle of Chanel cost $15–20. While they were moaning and groaning about what we did, I could not express my dislike of the smell I experienced. Much, much later in the United States, I was teaching piano and had a student who was a very accomplished pianist. She consistently wore a perfume that smelled similar to what we experienced in Crimea. I had to drop her as a student, and she couldn't understand why. I couldn't stand the smell anymore!

Leaving the peninsula was hasty and unorganized. We hurried to boats at the shore. These vessels were not equipped for war. Just before we docked on Romanian shores, the Russian planes dropped fire bombs on both ships, and they caught on fire. All the men got out, but all the equipment was lost and sank to the bottom of the sea. It was becoming evident that the Germans were losing the front line. We were falling apart. We had to get back to Berlin by crossing the Balkan states. The headquarter officers with all the documents were flown to Berlin, but we had to join any westward-moving units. The Bohemians had quite a few partisans. They were snipers supplied with Russian weapons and did a good job of disengaging the German units.

We managed to get together with some lost soldiers, eleven of us, with a sergeant as our leader. He told us to stay where we were and to wait for him. He came back with a horse and a small cart. We put some heavy stuff in the cart and started walking. We were getting tired. I was getting weak. We started taking turns holding one hand on the cart while walking. My turn came. I held on to the corner of the vehicle while walking, and I fell asleep. I even had a dream. It started to rain, and my turn was up. It was getting dark, and we were slowing down our pace. It had just stopped raining, and the sky was still touching our heads, the heavy boots stomping irregularly in the mud on the deserted road. Nobody dared to stop, even for a brief rest. Not one of us would have been able to stand up and continue. The small platoon moved along in such a way that an undertaker would have loved to see it.

We came across evidence of another platoon that looked like it had been in a fight with the partisans. There was no sign of life anymore. We heard a moan and found one German lieutenant wounded in the left leg and bleeding. The sergeant took his belt and tied it around the lieutenant's upper leg to stop the bleeding. We put him in the cart, and I noticed his bare leg hanging from the edge. The leg was cold, and it was exposed to the almost-freezing air. The bleeding seemed to have stopped and the blood wasn't streaming down anymore. The lieutenant was young. He looked down at his wound quite often and winced. The one in the front leading the horse stopped. We all looked up. A civilian was walking toward us. The man was small and his pace was slow. He was an old man. He tried to make way for us by stepping aside. The lieutenant saw him.

"Take him with us!" he cried out in a high-pitched voice.

We continued to move.

"I said take him!" His voice pierced through our backs.

The one in the front casually motioned the rifle toward the front, and the old man without any hesitation took his place in front of us. We moved on.

It was getting colder. A fresh stream of blood froze on the lieutenant's leg. The bleeding stopped. I listened to the sucking noise of our heels in the mud. It was different. It had a firmer sound than before. We had to find shelter. The darkness was taking over rapidly. It felt like another wave of rain was catching up with us. There was some uneasiness in the old man's action. He finally stopped and pointed over to a meadow. We could barely see it, but he knew there was an old shack there. As we got closer, we noticed that most of the roof was still on. One at a time, passing the door, we dropped on the floor to the closest empty spot. No one wanted food, we just lay there, exhausted and glad not to be getting wet. There is a time when one has almost given up, but on the verge of breakdown; he stops for a moment and catches a full breath — a breath that is penetrated with the taste of life. As we were resting there and not moving and not getting wet, it was a sign of life. We felt that we were still able to see each other. We lay there with closed eyes and no desire to talk — only tired happiness covered our faces.

There were only four eyes wide open in the darkness. The old man got up slowly, watching the lieutenant, and gathered some wood. There were wood chips in the center of the shack. Convinced that nobody had an objection, he started a fire. I opened my eyes.

How much time had elapsed? I looked at the lieutenant and the prisoner and they were wide awake. It was surprising how the prisoner watched the fire and the young lieutenant. I almost felt he had the desire to go over to him, change his bandage and comfort him.

The next time I woke up, the lieutenant was not at the same place. I looked at the prisoner and followed his eyes toward the corner which the lieutenant was crawling to. He finally reached the corner, pushed himself up onto his right foot and took down an old rope which was hanging from a nail. I was wide awake. I guessed what his plan was. I sat up and edged my neighbor. The lieutenant heard our movements, turned around, looked at the prisoner and in an almost crying voice, shouted, "I am going to hang you, you dirty partisan!"

We were all awake. In slow movement, all of us managed to stand up. I looked over at the prisoner and saw no change in his face. He was still looking at the lieutenant with the same expression as before. It took him quite a while to make a loop, throw the rope over a beam and drag an old box from the middle of the room.

The old man stood there, and I tried to put myself in his place. I didn't think he really cared what happened to him because he was that old. He was just concerned about us and our fate.

All of the sudden, I remembered my favorite readings of Alexandre Dumas' *The Count of Monte Cristo*, where the old man was serving his prison term and dreamt of getting out and becoming a happy man because had buried a large treasure chest on the island of Monte Cristo in the Tyrrhenian Sea. During his imprisonment he managed to contact a young man who was thrown in prison by a wealthy person just to prevent his union with a girl who the wealthy man was trying to keep for himself. Knowing that he was getting too old and would not make his dream come true, the old man helps the young to escape and guides him to the treasure.

I always believed that Dumas' story was a legend until later in my life I was visiting the city of Marseille, the capitol of Bouches-du-Rhône and was surprised to notice the tourist attraction "Visit the prison of the Count of Monte Cristo." I took the ferry to the prison and visited the place where the old man and the count dug the tunnel to each other's cell and planned the escape that created the famous story. I felt for the old man who was trying to help the young.

The lieutenant ordered the old man to get over there. He shouted to us, "Don't you men move. He is going to hang! He is a partisan."

The old man got on the box without any resistance.

"Let him go, lieutenant." A strong voice cut through the air. That was our sergeant. He slowly raised his rifle. The old man was trying to put his head into the loop and the lieutenant was getting ready to kick the box with his boot when a bullet ricocheted next to the box.

"Let him go," the sergeant repeated in a commanding tone. There was silence again. Now we heard sudden heavy raindrops on the roof. The old man's face did not look tired. The lieutenant slowly collapsed on the floor and we could hear his sobbing. The prisoner slowly freed himself from the noose and came out to the fire, put another log on it and walked out slowly into darkness.

The next day saved us all. A large German unit, equipped with vehicles, came by and we were saved. The unit was to move to Berlin and we were told to report where we belonged, to headquarters. I resumed my translation work when they needed me. We never heard about the lieutenant.

The news reports were getting more and more negative. D-Day was announced in June, which meant that Germans had to fight the East and West front at the same time. My job of translation almost stopped. The next bad news for me was that Russians were pushing deeper into the Balkan countries toward the German heartland. There was news of Russian troops fighting on the German side, being organized by Germans with the help of General Vlasov. He surrendered to the Germans and offered to use his division to fight against the Soviets. He was eventually captured by the Russians and hanged, of course, as a traitor.

Here I was, going to the prison camp, translating messages encouraging prisoners to join Vlasov's army. What will happen to me when the Russians come in? I worried about my future. I decided to try my luck and ask the member of the headquarters to help me get toward the west where the Russians could not reach — the Americans were supposed to capture the western part of Germany.

I had a hard time convincing the superior commanders who had the power to help me move west when the Russians were not present.

"We do not think they will do anything to you," they told me. "You were not fighting. You were just a translator. You didn't have any weapons. You don't have to worry." After I told my family's fate and me being the son of an enemy of the Soviet Union, they helped me and one of them went to the general's headquarters to get permission for me to move west. I received a very strong letter which said that "this person has to get to Salzburg and no transport should be denied. The matter is imperative for him to be there as soon as possible." That was a strong statement, and everywhere I showed my permit, I was given transportation to the west. I think all the work I did for headquarters was paying off. That was a way for them to say "thank you" by saving my life, and they did.

I was put in with some heavily wounded soldiers going to a hospital in western Germany. I got off in Salzburg. There was a sergeant guiding soldiers. I showed my papers.

"Wait here," he said. "I'll be relieved soon and you can come with me. Salzburg was declared a free city and Americans will be coming in soon. You are a translator and you could be helpful." I didn't bother explaining to him that I was good with the Russian language but not with English. We went to a hostel. The host was helpful and offered to help us get rid of our uniforms. He found some old clothing for us. We got rid of our uniforms and looked very funny in our Bavarian outfits. American troops rolled in on the third day with army trucks and tanks. Soldiers were throwing chocolates and cigarettes, and cheerful people greeted them in the streets. Everyone was joyful the war was over.

The next day, a jeep was going through the city with a loud-speaker. "All people who served in the German army, report to the army camp for discharge papers." We went and got in the line the next day. There were not many of us there. Our turn came. At the gate, a young American soldier asked us, "Deutsch Soldat?" The sergeant looked at me, expecting me to translate into English. I said to him that I translated Russian, not English. Oh my God, he looked terrible and troubled.

I tried to respond to the American soldier, "Ja, vi Deutsch soldat." He got excited and started to communicate with his body language and gesticulations to let us know what he was after. "Du uniforms? Du pistols?"

My friend responded with "Ja, ja, uniforms — in the river." He motioned with gestures to imitate the water. The soldier understood.

"Ich chocolate, cigarette — you show place, next day here you come."

We got the message. He wanted souvenirs. We told him we would come back. We had thrown all our outfits into the Salzburg River tied with our belts. The sergeant's pistol was heavy enough to sink all our belongings. Our dismissal was quick and painless. The sergeant got papers that he voluntarily reported himself for dismissal, I got my Displaced Persons papers, which were given to all non-German citizens, and the American soldier got his souvenirs. Life changed all of the sudden. I was a civilian and free. Our host gave me some work at the guesthouse in the kitchen, and I had a place to stay.

A month later, my host told me that there were Russians soldiers coming in the American zone with American trucks and announcing on the loud-speakers, "All people born in Soviet Union, come to the army camps. We will help you to go home." Now, that worried me. Two weeks later, the news spread that the Russians lined up the former Soviets and put them in the trucks and freight trains, for what destination where? Of course,

Siberia, prison, or who knows. I had to hide. My host helped me to join the lumberjacks high in the Bavarian Alps. My life changed again, but this time it was very different.

It was hard work, but good exercise, clean air, good food. I got stronger day by day. Food and books were our payment for cutting firewood for the top people in town. We were not paid with money. Our reimbursements were clothing, food, books and kerosene lamps to read by. The hut we stayed in was especially built for the lumberjacks, with a fireplace. It was quite comfortable. I gained all my muscles back and was getting lots of reading done. Our duties were to cut down the trees, but only the marked ones. I learned to admire the German foresting techniques.

The trees we were permitted to cut were too old, or they were too close together. They could not develop to a healthy stage. We had to cut them into one-meter lengths and organize them into a "Stier" — what the Germans call a pile. It had to be one meter deep, one meter high and one meter long. They called it "ein Stier" — the measurement of the unit. One "Stier" was enough for a family for two cold months to heat and to cook dinner. The only transportation for the people was horse

carts or sleighs in the winter. We had no power tools —
just two-man saws and large hammers and axes to scrape
the wood. It was great exercise for staying strong and
healthy, and we were that!

The forest inspector was a highly-educated
horticulturist. He would stay sometimes with us, and I
learned that he was not only a good forest ranger, but a
good chess player also. He would stay overnight and we
played several games of chess. Luckily for me, my dad
had trained me in chess in my younger years. Our cabin
was built very well as a log cabin and had good stoves to
cook and stay warm. We were able to use a library
indirectly. The customers would check out books for us,
and the forest ranger would take them back and also
check out new books for us. We had some great books to
read during the one-and-a-half years I spent up there.

The "Stier" wood piles had to be placed by the
mountain roads which were accessible to the horse carts
and sleighs. A year passed by and I was safe from being
kidnapped; then good news came. The chief of the U.S.
Armed Forces, General Eisenhower, stopped giving
permission to Russians to enter into American zones,
which meant that all the displaced persons were
protected. The reports used to come that some

kidnapped people had jumped from the trains or trucks to commit suicide. It was a great humanitarian move by General Eisenhower to stop this, which impressed me very much. My admiration for Americans was growing, and I decided to come down from the Alps and find some job.

There was a piano repair shop in Bad Reichenhall, a small Bavarian town. Herr Hock was the master piano technician, and when I told him my background, that I had studied piano, he hired me. I learned to tune and regulate the pianos. The best part of the job was that Herr Hock would let me practice as long as I liked after work.

Herr Hock showed me an announcement about the well-known Salzburger Mozart Festival.

"You know this is an important event. It stopped during the war, and it is going to start again with a great concert to renew the tradition."

I had heard so much about the Mozart Festival which attracted famous musicians. The program mentioned Mahler's works with Elizabeth Schwartzkopf, a famed soprano, in "Das Lied von der Erde."

"I would give anything to attend that performance," I exclaimed.

"You should know that people come from all corners of the world and tickets are expensive."

"Oh well, forget it — I can't get that kind of money." I was ready to walk out the door when he stopped me.

"I tell you what: you get three *Sters* of wood for my family and I'll see that you have a ticket."

"But how can you get one?"

"There are black marketeers there — you can get anything."

Three *Sters* (or cords) of wood was enough for a family to go through the winter — all I would have to do was work hard for two weeks. I felt like my dream was coming true.

I knew I couldn't depend on transportation in those days, so I would need to get there on foot. Salzburg was a half-a-day hike from Bad Reichenhall.

In two weeks Herr Hock had a ticket for me, and I faced another problem. He mentioned that people come in highly formal dress, but all I owned was my work outfit. However, one family had paid me with a very nice-looking lederhosen, a beautiful symbolic dress for Bavarian and Austrian mountaineers, with long socks coming up to my knees and leather suspenders with a wide leather brace across the chest incised with an Edelweiss flower, the emblem of a good hiker. I also had a nice long-sleeved white shirt I was saving for important occasions.

I put all my best clothes to show to Herr Hock. "Well, what do you think — do I pass?"

He measured me up and down. I looked very good, I thought.

"Your ticket is in the very last row of the auditorium. Wait till all people go in and then sneak in unnoticed. I do not think you should subject high society to your lederhosen."

Well... I did not care. I was going to hear and see something unforgettable.

Next day I started my hike early and was in Salzburg by the early afternoon hours. I looked up my old friend who had taken me in his hostel to shelter me and had sent me to the lumberjacks after the end of the war. I asked if I could stay overnight in his guest house, because of the late hour of the Mozart Festival.

"You are going in *that* outfit to the Mozart Festival??"

I nodded.

"Well, do you know what kind of people go to that event, and do you have a ticket?"

"Yes, I do. Thanks — so I'll see you later. If you are not up, I know the room where I used to sleep."

I went to the famous place, found a bench across the large courtyard and watched the parade of fantastically dressed people moving toward the concert hall.

What should I do? Should I wait longer...? I might be too late.

I decided to go in. I got close to the entrance door. A uniformed usher noticed me.

"What are you doing here, young man?"

I showed him the ticket and told him, "I am waiting till all the people are in — it is because of my dress."

I noticed a very warm sympathetic look. "What do you care about people?! Come on in — you have a ticket, and as far as I can see you will be a better listener than all these decorated guests!"

I had a protector, thank heavens. I still waited for the last bell and went in. I found my seat in the last row and luckily on the end of the row, so that I would not have to rub my lederhosen, which had distinct fumes of fresh leather, on the people who were already seated. Next to me was a couple, with the lady just next to me. I noticed her discomforted manner and sure enough she soon asked her husband to move next to me.

Bruno Walter came on stage, and from then on I thought of nothing but the orchestra, a dream orchestra. Gustav Mahler's works were not publicly performed during Hitler's regime and I had heard that Bruno Walter was a Mahler specialist, aside from being his close friend.

We could all feel the power of the unbelievable purity of the sound and phrases. Not just Herr Walter was all in his element, but the musicians seemed to be transplanted into another world, the world of Mahler. The incredible warmth of Frau Schwarzkopf's singing brought tears to my eyes. More than half a century later after that miraculous performance, I can close my eyes and relive the experience I had in Salzburg. The power of the music was contagious. The audience seemed to breathe with the sound. The final chord was barely finished when the entire audience leapt to their feet. The ovation would not stop.

I am sure that I was not alone in feeling elevated. The couple next to me, completely disregarding my appearance, shook my hand — my lederhosen were fully accepted — "Was this not a wondrous evening?" telling me almost in unison.

It was more than a concert. The dream of humanity to unite came through, thanks to the power of music. Next day I hiked back to Badreichenhall with a rekindled desire to get back to music.

My mind became occupied with finding a music school. Herr Hock showed me an announcement about the Munich Conservatory. The well-known Handel Conservatory was getting back in full swing. They were having auditions, and I decided to try my luck, even though my practicing was still in the beginning stages. The auditions were open to anyone who was at the conservatory-training level. The city of Munich was not too far and I took three days off to go and try my luck.

The day before the auditions, I visited the Georgian Immigration Association in Munich. They had more Georgians than Berlin. The next day I signed up my name for an audition and was scheduled for the same afternoon. Entering the audition room, I found myself quite nervous and afraid that after my five years of musical lapse, I would not be good enough to be accepted. In the testing room there was only one professor. Professor Zimmermann, a middle-aged, kind-looking man invited me to the piano. Reading my name, he asked, "What nationality are you?" I told him, and he was familiar with Georgia.

"What are you going to play for me?"

"I'll try Chopin's waltz in C sharp minor, but I have to tell you that I have not practiced for five years."

"What were you doing, young man?" I told my story as briefly as I could, but he wanted to know more. That gave me confidence to approach the piano. Maybe he just wanted to relax me. I played and made more mistakes than the last time I played.

"I see that you missed a long period of practicing, but there is something in your playing that I like. I like the way you relate one sound to the next. It makes the phrases very warm. Let us try one year and see what we can do. I'll take you as my student."

I was accepted. I went back to the Georgian Association to tell them the news. "You need a scholarship," they told me. A month later, I received a letter from the association that they would support me with a stipend. I started my long desire in life; I was a full-fledged student.

Prof. Zimmermann was a great teacher. After one year at the conservatory I was getting in good shape. I started to play like before. The Immigration Association turned out to be like a protective parent for me. I was informed by a neighbor that I had a relative in the United States — in Los Angeles, California — and the organization would be happy to get the address and make the contact. After some research, I found out about the Los Angeles Conservatory of Music and Art, and I decided to discuss the news with Prof. Zimmermann. He encouraged me to go for a year or two and see how much I could pick up there. The association's office arranged my screening and getting the affidavit for California as a displaced person. President Truman had signed a new bill allowing displaced persons to immigrate to America with a sponsorship from a U.S. citizen. Again, the association's office helped me to get my relative to sponsor me.

I also got help from an American officer who used to come play chess with us lumberjacks. This amiable gentleman completely understood why we were hiding in the forest. He spoke German well enough that we could converse with him, and he turned out to be a nature lover. He visited our camp several times. I had enough confidence in him to tell him my entire story. He was a great help to me in arranging my pass as a DP (displaced person) under President Truman's quota. He even drove me to Munich to the American immigration office. I went in to the screening committee but was refused because I said I had been an interpreter for the German army. When I came out, looking dejected, he asked what happened. I told him. He told me to go back in again, to a different agent, and not to say anything — just show my hands. He said soft hands were suspicious, but luckily for me, my palms were rough from being a lumberjack. This second time, I passed! After some tiresome check-ups and medical examinations, I received a visa to go to California. I said "auf Wiedersehen" to my Prof. Zimmermann and I was sailing to the dream land.

CHAPTER THREE:

AMERICA

"Though we travel the world over to find the beautiful,
we must carry it with us or we find it not."
Ralph Waldo Emerson, "Art"
(*Essays* (First Series, 1841), no. 12)

World War II was over and the increased number of displaced persons was becoming a concern for the European nations. When the USA opened the door with an immigration quota, it was a relief for the continent. Displaced persons' departure from Germany was from Bremerhaven, a very busy harbor. There were large vessels converted from war ships into transport ships. Our vessel's name was General Hershey, and there were 1,500 displaced persons with destinations for Canada (500), New York (500) and New Orleans (500). I was put in the New Orleans group, the so-called "South Group". There were all kinds of nationalities on the ship. I befriended a Hungarian couple who were musicians. We spent most of the time in our cabins and played bridge. There was a feeling of exuberation among the passengers. The word "America" had a special effect on all of us. When we did not play cards, I enjoyed staying on the upper deck.

Crossing the ocean had a hypnotic effect on me. I asked myself, how long will I be like a tumbleweed in this world? Will I find home in America? Will I be happy in my studies? All these kinds of questions were swimming in my head.

I watched intently the sea gulls traveling with us, wondering when they would fly back to Germany, to their homeland. After several days I started to worry that they may not make it back, since we were getting close to the half-way point. My friends, who had traveled over the ocean before, explained that sea birds knew when to leave the ship. They were right about that. In a couple of days they flew away, except three of them that kept sitting on the rail on the upper deck. Again, I was worried, but my friend assured me that birds who were sick knew that they would not make it back and it was safer to stay on the ship. I kept checking them every day and noticed that sailors would bring leftovers for them which they would gulp down. We were approaching Halifax, Canada, and the three sea gulls became Canadian citizens. They flew to the shore.

Approaching Halifax was like a dream. It is the most beautiful natural harbor in the world. It was full of small islands greeting us in the darkness and the dolphins with their gymnastic swimming accompanied us to the main harbor. We waved good-bye to the Canadian part of our passengers and sailed on down to New York. Everybody was on the top deck to see the Statue of Liberty, and again we wished good luck to the next 500 people. Then it was our turn. As we were approaching New Orleans harbor, the announcement came from the captain saying that if there is anything to be thrown off board, it was to be done before we crossed the tidal zone so that we did not trash and pollute the shores. I looked at my old jacket. It did not look very presentable. On top of that, to stand in front of my relatives, it would not present me the way I wanted to be presented. So I took it off and tossed it overboard, saying good-bye.

I arrived in America with two good-looking shirts. We stayed in the harbor and watched our cases lowered down with huge nets. Down below the workers made piles for us to pick up and go through customs. I had a fairly large, heavy case, well-packed and locked up. I noticed that when one worker tried to pick it up and found it heavy, he called for help and the two of them put it aside, away from the other piles. After going through customs and claiming my case, the officers asked me to open it. Two men put it in front of me and they all gathered around to watch me. I unlocked the padlock. I knew what they were expecting to see. I had heard that there were lots of people purchasing silver and gold service sets, vases and precious materials to bring with them. You should have seen their faces when I kept showing them sheets of music, books and scores.

"Are you a musician?"

I had enough vocabulary in English to say, "I... study... music... in... Los Angeles." They all had friendly faces and wished me good luck. I kept that strong zinc metal case to store my music for a long time, and later my son, Temmo, continued the same tradition.

We were put in different groups with different destinations. My group had to be housed for two days before our transportation. The papers and notifications to our sponsors had to be received before our departure. A guide was assigned to us to see the city of New Orleans, and I was mesmerized by the street musicians performing the most captivating sounds. At one place we passed a club of some sort where a beautiful combination of jazz passages was coming out. I had to stop and listen. My guide understood my excitement and waited by the open door. It was exciting! What an imagination, what a freedom of expressing the feelings in music. I fell in love with New Orleans-style jazz.

The third day came and we were at the railroad station getting in the cars. Our luggage was sent to our sponsors. We all got our tickets and I got into a car and noticed that the people in that car were all black, so I sat down next to one young boy. I was very surprised when the conductor came through and asked me to go to the next car. He motioned with his finger for me to go there. I thought he wanted me to be with some of the other people in my group, but I was comfortable where I was. An elderly black man asked me to please go with the conductor, not to make trouble. I got to the next car. What I saw bothered me very much. Everyone in that car was white. I could not understand. In my country, we didn't have many black people, but the ones we had, I remember, were very much admired. We even had a black fire department chief. He was an admirable man — tall and very handsome. He would sit on top of the fire truck during the parades, and people would wave and applaud. After I became an American citizen and found out that the racial separation was waning, I felt better. We traveled many hours. I found a place by the window next to a very friendly man. We approached a large city.

I reached for my pocket dictionary, which was getting crumpled edges already. After looking up the words, I asked my neighbor, "What is this?"

"Los Angeles," he said very slowly and pronounced. The train was slowing down.

"Thank you," I squeezed through my untamed vocal muscles. I still couldn't say the short "a" sound. It sounded more like "Thahnk you." My voice was trembling and I noticed my shaky hand when I reached for my baggage. I was excited, very excited. This was going to be my home. I thought of the letter from my friend Shota Margvelashvili, who had moved to Los Angeles before me, telling me not to be afraid when I arrived in the city.

The man must have noticed my uneasiness, for he tried to tell me that there was plenty of time and not to hurry. I didn't understand, but replied properly with, "Thahnk you."

I sat close to the window and watched the houses with solid walls. I tried hard to relate them to the walls we used to see when we rode the train in our home town. They never looked clean, and all they did was ricochet the sound of the train. These walls were different. They were painted all over with nice looking ladies with pretty legs. They were all smiling. It was fascinating.

We were travelling for almost half an hour through the city and I was convinced the train wasn't going to stop in Los Angeles. We must have passed it. I took my wrinkled dictionary again and asked the same question. The man smiled and said, "Los Angeles."

More pretty girls on the walls. Some of them were dressed quite fine. One was holding toilet paper in her hand. I couldn't figure out why she should have on such a fine dress to hold toilet paper.

More houses. We were still travelling through the city. The man couldn't stand my anxiety and tried to show me how big Los Angeles was by stretching his hands as far as he could. He motioned for me to sit back and relax by doing so himself. Being afraid I would make him uncomfortable by standing up in front of the window, I spent the next fifteen minutes in a reluctant position imitating him.

The train came to a stop. I was the first to get off. It smelled so different from our railroad station at home. It smelled like Christmas, although it was June. Christmas was the only time we used to make popcorn at home and brew coffee.

I knew my friend was not going to be there, but I still looked for him. How will I find my friend's house? With that fear I reached in my pocket to find the most valuable piece of paper I possessed. It was still there.

Three, seven, nine East C. Street. I almost knew it by memory.

Somebody tapped me on the shoulder. My travelling companion was smiling at me, and it felt like I found an old friend again. He spoke several long sentences, using his hands and eyebrows, but I did not understand. Finally, in despair, he repeated one word, "Address, address." I knew what "address" was and showed my old, yellow paper to him. He motioned for me to follow.

I felt people looking at us. It must have been my dress. I would have to dress differently here. Or it could be my mustache. Thunder struck me. In a panic, I looked around to find at least one person with a mustache. Not one had the slightest shadow on the upper lip. But shaving one's mustache means losing one's manhood. How could I face my friends? People were still looking at us with curiosity. This time I was convinced it was the mustache. I don't know how long we walked. I didn't know anything. My thoughts were occupied with shaving the mustache.

"Taxi," I heard my friend calling.

The yellow car pulled up in front of us. After talking to the driver for a little while, he opened the car in the back, shook my hand, spoke to me, and closed the door tightly after me.

It took me months to get over my taxi ride. I didn't know how he managed to take me to my friend's house, going through so many streets and between so many cars.

My friend Shota was very well-adjusted for only having been here one year. He had a little apartment with a kitchen. The kitchen smelled of familiar food that made me hungry for the first time since I left the ship in New Orleans.

"You look so young, like an American," I said.

"After you get rid of your mustache and put new clothes on, you will look like a young American too."

I still felt like keeping my mustache. I am a Georgian after all.

I asked Shota to take me to my relatives. He seemed to know about them. We Georgians have a peculiar habit. We do not often like to live in close colonies in exile. We are like eagles, and creating colonies is not in our blood. We live apart, but stay in touch with each other. Shota told me about them, and he knew that they were waiting for me. We changed several street cars and knocked on the door of my relatives. It was a beautiful two-story house in the foothills of Griffith Park.

The welcome was like a wish come true. They showed me a room and said it was my room, and there was a grand piano in the living room. They taught me how to take the streetcar to downtown LA where my conservatory was located, at the corner of Figueroa and 8th Street. They helped me to register at the school, where I continued my habit of attaching myself to my teachers as if I was searching for my father and mother.

In a sense, most of my teachers were replacing my parents. I found mentors again. At the conservatory I was helped by Mary Louise Williams, a great pianist and a great teacher; Mr. Earle Voorhies; and then Dr. Oscar Wagner. Dr. Wagner was German and that made my life easier. He had been head of the Juilliard piano department and then decided to open a music conservatory in Los Angeles. I lucked out again. My studies started to go well. However, I was facing a big problem. My relatives' grand piano was in the living room and they told me it was for me. They never touched the instrument. In the conservatory the practice rooms were busy. You had to sign up, and the maximum practice time was 1–2 hours. I did not worry because I had the piano at my relatives'. I started to put in 3–5 hours of practice at home, but my dream did not last long. Here came the doomsday.

My relatives were getting a little tense, I noticed. My aunt's husband had a talk with me. They could not listen to my practice all day and asked if there was another place for me to work. I started to worry. My English-language lessons were at the Hollywood High evening school. I was doing quite well, but not enough to find a place to live. I asked Mr. Earle Voorhies at the music school, and he explained to me that the seniors had priority for using the practice rooms. That was the rule, and he didn't have any advice for me. That evening I went to my English-language school at Hollywood High and shared my problem with my friend. Walter was a middle-aged immigrant from Germany working as a chauffeur for a well-known movie actress, Janet Gaynor. He used to tell me how nice his employer was. She helped him and his wife come to America. The wife was a cook for the family, and Walter was in charge of transportation. Walter was trying to comfort me, but I still had the feeling that I should go back to Germany.

"I am going to talk to my wife. Maybe she can asked Mrs. Gaynor what can be done," he said. Good old

Walter. They both talked to Janet about my misfortune. She said she loved music, and she would like to see me. I stopped practicing at my relatives', and I told them I was able to practice at the school. I didn't want to complicate our relationship. The next day at school, Walter told me that Mrs. Gaynor would like to see me. I put my best shirt on, shaved, bought a nice bouquet of flowers, and when Walter drove me to a beautiful continental villa in Bel Air, we rang the bell and Janet Gaynor opened the door. I presented my bouquet and kissed her hand. When we went into the large, beautiful living room, I was ready to impress her with my playing. I asked, "Where is your piano?" She gave me a beautiful, embarrassed and disarming smile. I was falling in love with her. She had the most beautiful eyes I'd ever seen.

"I do not have a piano."

I almost shouted back, "You — you don't have a piano?!"

Another devastating, disarming smile again and she said, "Don't worry, my dear young man. I have a grand piano in my beach house in Playa del Rey, which we do not use much any more, and you are more than welcome to live there and practice as much as you like. The house is deserted, but that will suit you best."

Again, I felt that an angel was guiding my steps. I moved into her empty beach house. The swimming pool was filled with sand and was never used. The grand piano needed a little work, which I did myself. The kitchen was in great shape. I learned to cook my own dinner and breakfast. I could practice day or night — no close neighbors. Even at midnight I would practice until I got tired and was beautifully lulled to sleep by the tireless lullaby sung by the ocean waves. Once in a great while, the Gaynors and some friends would come to the beach house to play bridge, and if I was home, they would ask me to play the piano for them. I started to have a great audience, and I enjoyed playing for them.

I was finishing my second year when I realized that I should have another job to meet some expenses. I needed some more income. When I mentioned to my student friends, one of them, who was from South America, advised me to go to the employment office. "You have been in America more than a year. You took out your first paper to apply for citizenship, didn't you?" he asked. I said that I had. I put in my first papers because my teachers had advised me to do so, but I was not sure that I was going to apply for citizenship and I was not sure whether I would stay here or go back to

Germany. Then he told me how he got a nice job at a furniture company helping to mix paint.

I decided to go to downtown LA to the unemployment office as he suggested. I got in line and at the window a very jovial and happy-looking African-American woman asked me, "How can I help you, honey?" I felt comfortable with the way she called me "honey," and I told her my problem.

"So you are a student and need some income. Well, I have a job you can try. There is a nice large, fine, fancy Mayflower Coffeehouse on Hollywood Boulevard. They make wonderful doughnuts. They need a man at the window to fish them out from the fry-oil with tongs and put them on the conveyor belt behind the large window so that the pedestrians can watch the doughnuts go by on the belt, just to arouse their appetites. They will give you a white coat and a tall white hat. You have a nice mustache and should look pretty handsome. Would you like to do that?" She made the job sound as jovial as she was. I could not say no.

"Yes, I would like to try that," I answered and got the address and the necessary papers. I went there to watch the work. The coffeehouse was right on the boulevard and as she said, lots of pedestrians stopped to watch the old man taking out the doughnuts and putting them on the conveyor belt. I went in and presented my papers. The manager had a nice, convincing manner.

"Just watch him for a while and you will do the same thing tomorrow. The man is moving away and you will have his job."

So I watched for an hour and I thought it was easy and the hours were right. The next day I started the job. I put my white apron and tall white hat on. I thought, what would my teachers and musician friends say if they saw me in such a "non-musical" outfit, but it was fun. The best part was when young, beautiful girls would stop and watch me. I enjoyed that best and found myself communicating with my eyes with them. The problem was that by looking for too long at them, some doughnuts would burn. The manager told me, "You can take the burned ones home with you. But try to be more careful."

Things did not improve very much. The pretty girls kept stopping and doughnuts kept burning. One nice thing about burning doughnuts was that going home I had at least a variety of one dozen burned ones that did not taste too bad. I started to give them to little boys on my street and word got out. These little bike riders were circling near the streetcar stop. They knew the exact time to be there for my arrival. I would hand the bag to one of them and they had a good party on their circling bikes. The job was OK, but I got fired. The burned doughnuts were actually not the reason I got fired. The reason was much worse.

The manager, who seemed to enjoy my being there, came to me one afternoon and asked, "After you change, before you go home, take this bundle of mail across the street and put it in the blue mailbox." That seemed easy. I took the bundle of letters and went across the boulevard. In those days, the streets used to have two same-sized blue boxes: one was mail and the other was for trash. Being in a hurry to catch my streetcar and not knowing the difference between the boxes, I put the bundle in the wrong one: in the trash. A week later, the manager approached me with his palm on his chin.

"Did you mail my package last week?"

"Yes, I did."

"Let's go over and you show me where you put it." We went and I showed him the exact box.

"Oh my gosh, you got me in big trouble." That was a strong lesson for me. I knew exactly which was the mail and which was the trash from there on! But I did lose my job. He was trying to be friendly and told me, "Next time you have a job like this, don't watch the girls — watch the doughnuts."

"How can a young man watch doughnuts and not look at the girls?" I said to myself. I told him thank you, sorry and good-bye.

My studies continued to progress quite well. I was finishing my third year and my teacher, Mrs. Williams, asked me if I would enjoy listening to Dr. Wagner's student recital at his house.

"Dr. Wagner is asking about you periodically and he will be happy to see you," she told me.

The recital was very interesting and exciting. I grew closer to Dr. Wagner. Mary Louise Williams recommended me to him to tune his pianos. When I was in his house finishing tuning, we got to talk about my studies. He was very complimentary with my progress. I mentioned that I was homesick for Germany, and I had a continuing scholarship there, but if I stay here I have to work for my living, which would slow down my studies.

"If you worry about making a living, I have a solution for you. I, too, used to miss Germany, but I am happy I decided to stay and put my roots here." He came up with an offer which changed my life. "I can give you enough piano students, which will help you support yourself. But before you make the decision, I want you to know that next summer we have a great pianist from New York to teach our master class. You may enjoy observing her. She is from Russia, and you could talk to her about your future. I am sure she will excite you."

The summer came and the piano department was engrossed in preparation for her master class. Her name was Rosina Lhevinne. The day came when we were told to go to the assembly to meet her. After she was introduced to us, she got right down to business.

She wanted to know how many pianists were in the master class, and the first session was set for the next day. That day I took courage, and when she was going toward the master class room, I greeted her in Russian. She stopped, looked at me and said, "Are you Russian?"

"No, I am Georgian." I will never forget her expression. It made me feel so at home.

"Oh, I love Georgia and Georgians." She embraced me like a mother.

"My husband Joseph Lhevinne used to teach in Tbilisi. I love Tbilisi."

I did not know how to respond. I was overwhelmed with her friendliness.

"It is great to have you here," I said.

"Are you in master class?"

"No, not yet."

"See me again. I have to hurry." She pushed through the room with lots of energy.

At home I thought of the Tbilisi Conservatorium and all of a sudden the name Lhevinne came to me. My mother had told us how excited she was listening to the new Russian pianist Prof. Joseph Lhevinne, from Moscow, who captured the hearts of the conservatory with his recitals. I remembered how Mom was exuberant talking about his phrasings. "The warmest and unbelievably beautiful sounds he was able to produce." I was happy that I recalled the name Lhevinne and decided to see her again. Next day I waited in front of the classroom.

"Come with me. I am in a hurry." I kept up with the pace and told her about my mom.

"Mom has never missed any concerts of Mr. Lhevinne. She was crazy about his warm interpretations."

"I am so glad to hear that. Come in the room. You are welcome to listen." We walked in the room. The three master students looked nervous. The first student was from Israel. I knew him. I often listened to his practice and admired him. Here is what went on in front of me.

The student was studying Mozart's Concerto No. 24 in C major. Right at the opening statement Mrs. Lhevinne jumped out of her chair and said, "What are you telling me? Mozart did not mean those crescendos at the end of phrases. Let us try again." She would sing; she would use body language; she would play to demonstrate. It was a dynamic hour. By the time the student finished the first movement, he sounded great.

Some tempting thoughts were going through my head. Should I stay another year to have the same experience? But my mind was made up. I was going to be a teacher.

I was mesmerized. I was eating up every word and interpretation of hers.

After the last student, she turned to me.

"Let us talk about you. You started playing in Tbilisi and now you are in the L.A. Conservatory. Tell me how you got here." I told my story as briefly as I could.

"What are you working on now?"

"I started Mozart Sonata in A major."

"Play the opening theme for me."

I felt like I was recruiting all my performing abilities, and I played the theme.

"Did your mother advise you in some phraseology?"

"Yes, she did without failure."

"You have a very expressive touch. I hope you'll work up to the master class for next summer. I would love to hear you."

We parted as good friends. What I picked up from her lasted my whole life in my teaching career. I did not try for her master class, but I know that her ideas were transferred to my students.

I was getting involved in my private music students and often caught myself repeating Rosina Lhevinne's methods. I found that if I got upset, excited and emotional by hearing wrong notes or poor phrases, the effect was astonishing. Students started to be more alert and accurate. Rosina used to explode with a poor passage or phrase. My emotions put me in a very amusing case.

I had a high school senior, young, talented pianist. Once he picked up a difficult etude to study.

"I do not think you can master that piece. You need much more technique to play it," I advised him. Later we became good friends, and he invited me to his home. In our conversations, he told me that he was very seriously involved in gymnastics. I told him my stories about being in gymnastics in my school years. We were talking about single and double bars. I mentioned that I had a great teacher who taught me how to make a secure handstand without falling over. He got very excited.

"Can you still make one now?"

"I think I can still do it."

"Would you do it for me?"

I thought, I may use the occasion to persuade him to drop the difficult etude. An unforgettable thing happened.

He replied, "If I bring the etude perfectly, would you make the handstand on our high fence?"

I looked at the fence which was very high and could not help recalling my high school days. On Sundays we used to go to a park just to fool around. There was a tall bridge, where I used to make handstands to show off. Next to the bridge was a fine Italian ice cream parlor. Once I was asked to make the handstand on the rail of the bridge. There were some girls nearby. I made a daring stand while some elderly ladies were coming out of the parlor. They saw me stretch up and pleaded, "Oh my God, please tell him to come down. He may fall over. Please…please."

One of my friends replied, "Ma'am…he won't come down until we get him some ice cream."

"Oh, here, take this and buy some ice cream for all of you. Please hurry."

I came down, and we had enough money to invite the promenading girls.

I told my story to my student and his family, and it happened.

"If I bring the etude in perfect shape, would you make the handstand on our fence? We have a tall ladder."

I thought, why not make him practice hard. He won't make it anyway.

In two weeks he played the piece perfectly and I made the handstand. The family took the picture which I still keep to remind myself that if a student is motivated, he can do some wondrous things.

I was still playing recitals, but my teaching was taking over.

In further meetings with Dr. Wagner, I mentioned to him that my future as a concert pianist would deprive me of what I really wanted to do, namely to teach and raise musicians. After some thinking, he said, "Why don't we just think about a university where you can get the credentials to teach."

He thought highly of Santa Barbara. He knew Dr. Gillespie, who was the head of the music department and piano program. After some discussions with my teachers, we decided on UC Santa Barbara. The conservatory helped me to send recommendations to UCSB Music Department. I went up and met Dr. Gillespie. I played for him, and he was very happy to accept me as a music major in piano.

"We will see how many units we can transfer from the conservatory. I think you will be asked to cover more academic subjects," he said. He also informed me that President Truman signed a new bill which was that all displaced persons who immigrated to the US could enter the university without documentation as long as they met two requirements: 1) you had to pass the entrance exam; and 2) you had to maintain a B-average the first year of study. Nobody had papers from behind the Iron Curtain during that period, so this was great news. The graduation records were not obtainable from the Soviet Union.

A thousand thoughts crossed my mind: what about the masterclass, about Europe? Will I stay here for the rest of my life? I decided to stay. I did not have a homeland anymore and I needed a home. I knew that I could not go back. I shared my thoughts with Shota.

"You have to stay. I think you'll be happier here. Now you are going to Santa Barbara and you need a car." That was an exciting suggestion. During my jobs and teaching privately, I accumulated enough money to buy a car. I never learned or bothered and did not know how to handle my savings. I thought that if I returned to Europe I would just exchange my savings. I kept my money in a drawer where I kept my shirts, socks and underwear.

"Let us count how much you have," said Shota. There was $1,850.

"That is enough," he said. "There is a car dealer on Hollywood Boulevard – Gordon Chevrolet – and the cars are good. Let's go there." Shota already had a car, also a Chevrolet.

We went to the large car display window. As we started to walk around the display, I noticed that the salesmen were watching us intently and walking in the same direction as we were. It reminded me of my zoo visits where some animals would follow in the same directions as I was walking, maybe expecting treats.

"Let's go in," Shota decided. The salesmen were right there to open the door. My English was fair enough to communicate about the most important matters.

"How much for this green Chevy?"

"It is $1,680 plus tax."

Shota wanted to know what the total was. It turned out all in all to be not much over $1,800. Shota wanted to take it out for a drive and they were happy to go along. I had the feeling they were not taking us very seriously. We drove around a couple of blocks and Shota seemed to be pleased. He asked me in Georgian how I felt about the car.

"Oh, yes, I like it, if you approve," I answered. The salesman was puzzled.

"What language are you speaking?" he asked. When we explained, he said he had never heard of Georgian.

"How are you going to finance the car?"

"We pay money," I answered. He seemed puzzled. Shota asked to start on the ownership papers while I started emptying my pockets. One salesman disappeared in a hurry. I noticed in the small room more salesman got on their phones. The thought crossed my mind that they were calling local banks to see if anyone had been robbed. I finished counting and after the transaction was finished, we got into the car. The entire staff watched us drive off. We honked and they waved enthusiastically. As Germans say, "If the end is good, all is good."

I had a car and I had to learn how to drive. Shota's apartment was in a fairly quiet neighborhood and we started to practice. I'll never forget how concerned and worried Shota was when I was at the wheel. If there was a car coming toward us, he would lean out of the car window and very dramatically motion to the coming car to pull over so we wouldn't collide. His arm gestures were so emotional that the drivers would immediately pull over and that made my passing much easier. You should have seen their faces when I was passing by. We kept doing that for over a week until he thought that I was ready to pass the test. I do not know how, but I became a good driver and I had my own car.

I moved to Santa Barbara and took the entrance exam. I was amazed. I found that I passed the English language part of the exam, which was the hardest. If you failed, the college would still take you and enroll you into "bonehead" English. Sometimes I wished that I would have failed because I could have used the "bonehead" English at the beginning! I was very surprised when I picked up my results. I passed everything, including English, and I became a student at UCSB. I knew that I had to work hard to maintain the required B-average the first year. My efforts paid off, and studies were going fine, except for one misfortune.

To meet the academic requirements, I had to take science courses. I chose to take biology. I heard such great things about Dr. Harding, who was involved in the world population problem and was highly respected in the academic world. I was eager to do well, but no luck. In my mid-term exams, I failed, which meant that I could not maintain a B-average and I would lose my student status. His assistant, my lab instructor, noticed that I was upset and withdrawn.

"What's wrong with you?" he wanted to know. I showed him my test. Most answers were wrong. The test was about classifying a beaver. The reading I did said that they lived in water, so I classified them as a fish.

"We did not have beavers in our country," I said to him.

"Oh my God!" He explained to me what a beaver was. He brought out a biology textbook to show me the picture. We could not find any pictorial description of the beaver in the book. The incident was delivered to Prof. Harding. The next day I was told to go to Dr. Harding's office. I had the same heartbeat as I did in Munich for my auditions at the conservatory. I knocked at his door.

"Come in," a soft, kind voice told me. He looked at me silently. Then, "I owe you an apology. I know you don't have beavers in your country, and I should have had a picture in my textbook. Would you forgive me, and would you take another test? My assistant told me about you, and he will supervise during your exam." I took a deep breath and tried to control my happy tears. He noticed.

"What is your major?"

"Music, sir. I'm a pianist."

"Do you perform some recitals?"

"Yes, we have semester recitals in Dr. Gillespie's class. I'm majoring in piano."

I flew to my friends to deliver my news. My midterm was a success. I scored an A–, and the most beautiful thing was that when I entered the recital room, there was Prof. Harding in the first row. I played like an angel for him.

He approached me after the concert. "I like the way you interpret your music. All the muses were present in the room."

"Thank you so much for coming to my recital."

"You know, I have two boys. Would you come to my house and see if you can get them interested in piano lessons?" I knew I had another key person in my life.

We became good friends. When I visited him, he told me how he trained his boys to help him organize his publications. The written sheets were all over the room and the boys were giggling and accurately making sure that the right paper would go in the right pile. Our friendship grew with unexpected developments. Dr. Harding was quite involved and concerned about the government's role in the population explosion abroad, particularly in India. He tried to persuade politicians to help control the exploding problems. He asked to have discussion groups, and since I was taking a philosophy class by one of his colleagues, Dr. Gravetz, they invited some students to sit in on the discussions. I was honored to be included, and there I met Margaret Mead, who was persuaded to go to India and visit Gandhi to discuss the population explosion. Dr. Harding planted another seed in my life, and that was universalism. If we do not include the entire earth's population problems with our lives, we may harvest some trouble in our times. I remember his words. It is like a boat loaded to its fullest capacity to stay above the water, and if some more people hang on the side of the boat to climb in, then everybody will drown. I still use his words in my humanities class in my teaching.

I was becoming more confident in my studies. In the second year, I decided to take a very popular class by Dr. Marvin Mudrick. He was offering English literature. I knew that my command of the language was not ready, but what I was hearing about his teaching was enticing to me. I gathered the courage, and I signed up for his class.

Oh, dear! My first quiz was a disaster. He did not even grade the paper. He asked me what my nationality was and what language I was raised with. I told him I was Georgian, and that was my mother tongue. I also speak and have command of two other languages: Russian and German. "Oh that's right. Georgian is one of the ancient languages, isn't it?" I knew he was going to ask me whether I thought I should be in his class. He shook his head and said, "Well, we'll try it again."

We did a mid-term, and after seeing my paper, he called me in for a conference. "You have improved in your spelling, but I would advise you not to sign up for my class next semester." For the finals, I had the courage to ask him if he would give me an extra hour to finish my papers in his office. He did. I took another hour to write while he was correcting class papers. Alas, I barely made the class with a C– or D+ and he wished me good luck, but asked me please not to enroll in any more of his classes.

I do not know if it was my pride or my Georgian stubbornness. I worked hard on my English language. I was falling in love with the beautiful flexibility of it. I used to compare it to German. English was like an octopus. The definitions would not stop with one or two expressions, but would extend and give you an opportunity to express the idea. The new semester started, and I signed up for another class with him. I walked in his classroom, and he saw me sitting there. He shook his head and didn't say anything. The first big assignment was a short story. I remember Mrs. Vardiashvili, my literature teacher in Georgia. I felt challenged and worked hard, and I just let myself express my ideas and feelings. I handed my story in and felt like I was sitting on hot coals for two days. He came in the classroom and handed out papers. I read his comments one hundred times. "You did very well in telling the story. I like it. See me." Wow! I put my best shirt on and went to his office hours.

"Have you written much in your language?"

"Yes, I have." I told the story about my Georgian literature teacher.

"Well, would you forget what I said the first semester? I think you should write more." By the end of the semester, Marvin and I became friends. He never missed my recitals and published two of my stories in his department papers. Again, I gained another mentor. We stayed in contact many years after my graduation.

I wanted to pick up another instrument in my studies at UCSB. The viola was always attractive to me. I thought I would try the string instruments. Since I had to have a secondary instrument for my teaching credential, I decided to see Prof. Stefan Krayk, the head of the string program, to let me play a string instrument. He looked at me for a while and said, "Play viola." I started lessons with Prof. Krayk. His teaching was very strange and unusual. He introduced me to the viola.

"Just pick it up and put it under your chin and draw across the open string." First I thought he was joking, but I sensed that he was waiting for the terrible results which he received. I drew the bow across the strings and he said, "That doesn't sound good, does it."

"No," I said.

"Try it again. Remember the bow is the one that sets the sound and the vibration." I tried over and over again trying to make a better sound. He would not tell me how, just waited. He wanted me to find my own good sound. I did it again.

Finally, I took courage and said, "Would you please let me listen to a good sound?" He put the beautiful viola on his chin, and I heard the most beautiful sound.

"Try it again." This went on for half an hour. Finally, I took the instrument home and I practiced without interruption for a long time, until my landlord asked me politely if I would go to the garage and practice there. Prof. Krayk had me playing viola in four weeks so that I could get a simple line with the quartet with the other beginners. Oh my, we did not sound good, but by the end of the semester we had improved. I was surprised by the sound we started to get out of our instruments. I loved the viola sound, and being partial to the string instruments, I decided to buy one.

I was not too far in age difference from Stefan Krayk. We were both immigrants, he from Poland and I from Georgia. I started sharing some of my stories with him. I told him that I received my second papers for citizenship and I had to miss one of his classes to take my exams and receive my papers at the Santa Barbara courthouse. Stefan asked me to see him when I got back. He had a surprise for me.

At the courthouse I was questioned about the constitution and American history by some young law students. I was well prepared and when the judge noticed that I was eager to respond to the questions he turned to the young lawyers and said, "You better watch out. He may know more than you think."

The judge was just about to sign my citizenship documents when he stopped and looked at me and said, "Son, your name is extremely long, Wachtang Botso Chikvinidze. There are some twenty letters there. You'll have some problems. Don't you have another name?"

"Yes, I do. My father was a drama actor and he took Korisheli as his stage name."

"God bless." He turned and wrote on my documents "name to be changed to Korisheli."

I got back to school and looked up Stefan Krayk. I got his violin and played the American national anthem and he took me out to lunch.

He soon asked me if I would play some tennis with him as his partner on the courts. He turned out to be a tennis star, and I started to improve my strokes under his suggestions. I finally took courage and asked him again. "How is it that you let me figure out the good tone production on the viola on my own, and here on the tennis courts you give me such detailed instructions?"

"Ah," he replied. "Tennis is reflex, muscle coordination, good eye. Music is in your heart, in your blood, in your flesh, in your bones, it has to come from inside of you." I was amazed with his teaching methods. To play the instrument, you have to go through all kinds of readjustment of your natural postures, but Mr. Krayk started with the sound. Let me hear a beautiful sound. Why does it sound scratchy? Think about what causes the sound. He would demonstrate, and you would imitate, so step by step he was putting you in a position that was inescapable. You had to get a good sound first. I could not help but tell him that his method reminded me of the tribal people who were domesticating the elephant herds with a very natural kind of original way. First they build a fort near a big herd, then they cut bushes to hide themselves from the elephants, and then slowly — very slowly — they moved in a semi-circle in front of the herd. Of course, the elephants did not expect the bushes to move slowly to persuade them to enter the fort. As soon as they had the elephants inside the fort, they would close the gates quickly and the training would start after that. That reminded me that Stefan was kind of a tribal trainer and we had a good laugh about that! "OK, then I will be the tribal person and you will be my elephant. Do not forget that the more beautiful sound you get from your instrument, the more it will help you to find your soul."

Stefan had raised many famous string players and he was the founder of the Santa Barbara Symphony Orchestra — a great mentor. After I started my own orchestra, he used to visit me in Morro Bay and became the concert master of my house concert chamber orchestra. We all kept learning so much from him.

Botso, Age 4

Susana Bezhanishvili
Botso's mother

Platon Korisheli,
Botso's father

Platon Korisheli in Georgian drama, *Anzor.*
Sandro Akhmeteli, director (behind)

116

Working Unit, 1941 (Botso, second from left)

Ship that brought Botso to America

Botso in Los Angeles, circa 1950

Botso at Janet Gaynor's beach house, Playa del Rey.

University of California, Santa Barbara College

THE COMMITTEE ON DRAMA, LECTURES AND MUSIC

and

THE DEPARTMENT OF MUSIC

present

Wachtang Korisheli

in a

Senior Piano Recital

WEDNESDAY EVENING, MAY 15, 1957

8:30 P.M.

MUSIC BUILDING, CHORAL ROOM

PROGRAM

Sonata in D minor	*Scarlatti*
Sonata in E major	*Scarlatti*

∞∞∞

Sonata in D minor, Op. 31, No. 2	*Beethoven*
Allegro	
Adagio	
Impromptu in A flat major, Op. 90	*Schubert*

Intermission

La Cathedrale Engloutie	*Debussy*
Two Fantastic Dances, Op. 1	*Shostakovich*
Berceuse, Op. 57	*Chopin*
Leyenda	*Albeniz*

119

The handstand I promised my student

Temmo, Pat, Tina, Botso
in our Morro Bay Studio

Morro Bay heard in L.A. Wachtang Korishell directs the Morro Bay Elementary School Band while Yorty, mayor of Los Angeles, tunes in. The Morro Bay youngsters are to southern California this week and Tuesday performed at the City Hall in Angeles before moving on to the new Music Center where they were also h
(UPI teleph

Pelican sculpture and chessboard for
Morro Bay Centennial Stairway, 1977

Sophomore Gale Edgar wields a big drumstick.

The secret weapon

"The idea of the drum is similar to the Trojan Horse," says Morro Bay High School band director Wachtang Korisheli. "We hope it will give the team spirit, and maybe scare the other team a little."

The 6-foot drum, costing more than $1,000, is rolled out for football games and with the help of the class of '72 and the community, according to Korisheli who says the drum was built locally.

The stainless steel and plastic drum is mounted on a trailer which requires four to pull it. Korisheli says it has an "impressive, deep, handsome sound," and requires one man standing on either side

122

Orchestra Rated Superior

This year the orchestra consisted of 15 members. They played in 16 concerts and were judged in a S.L.O. Concert Competition in which they received a superior mark. They also went on a concert tour in Santa Barbara which was quite enjoyable.

The highlight of the year was when Karen Baillie, Lydia Hampp, and Anna Carey were chosen as All State Orchestra members.

Page 128. 1. Dr. Korishelli in his Sunday best. 2. Anna Carey jams on her cello. 3. *Orchestra: FRONT ROW*: A. Carey, K. Cannon, S. Garza, L. Hampp, D. Sakamoto, S. Quintana, A. Geiger. *MIDDLE ROW*: M. Dunn, J. Debacker, K. Baillie, P. Whelen, P. Debacker, B. Geiger, A. Galvez. *THIRD ROW*: Dr. Korishelli, Z. Schwass.

Georgian shepherds

Svaneti region, Georgia

Margaret in Georgia

Susana Bezhanishvili's grave

Botso's classmates, 1938 (Bosto middle row, 2nd from left)

Reunion with classmates, 1991 (Botso back row, left)

Dick and Botso on a hike   Platon as 'Vazha Pshavela'

Botso's Cove, San Simeon, California

George Papashvily   Helen Papashvily

Botso at George's grave

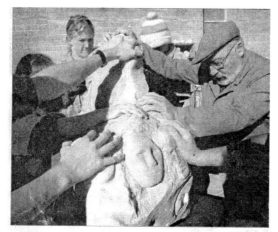

'IN MEMORIAM INNOCENTIUM': Mission Prep art instructor Wachtang Korishell, right, and h
students move their 1,200-pound sculpture Thursday. They will send it to Oklahoma City.

Mission Prep spends year on Oklahoma sculpture

Memorial sculpture for Oklahoma bombing, 1995

Installing the Morro Bay entrance sculpture, 2008

Kent Nagano, Botso. and Mari Kodama (Kent's wife)

Botso with Nancy Nagano

Botso and Margaret with their sculptures

Korisheli children:
Tina, Conlan (grandson,) Temmo, Ellena, Lia

Chapter Four:

Morro Bay

"Blessed is he who has found his work;
let him ask no other blessedness."

Thomas Carlyle, *Past and Present*, III:11

After graduation from UCSB, my request was to be placed in a public school to raise young musicians. I was given four addresses north of Santa Barbara in San Luis Obispo County. Taking my little Volkswagen, I started my journey. I found the San Luis Obispo school, and it turned out to be a high school which did not interest me. I was drawn to younger students. So I continued farther up north to a town called Atascadero, also beautifully located. Again, it was another high school. I went on to the next offer. The gas station directed me to drive the most beautiful road called Vineyard Drive over the hills to the coastal town of Cambria. The high school was located outside the town. I saw the beautiful building and what attracted me the most to this school was the football field covered with cattle grazing peacefully <u>on the field</u>. That was an unusual sight and I was curious. Even though it was a high school, I decided to go in. The secretary was very cordial and invited me to sit down and wait for the principal. Her manner encouraged me to ask, "How is it that the football field is a grazing place for the cattle?"

"Oh, well, the football practice does not start for a couple weeks and the cattle are doing a good job mowing the grass."

"What is the principal's name?"

"Mr. Hornaday. He has stepped out for lunch. If you would like, you can go for lunch and come back in an hour. You must be Mr. Korisheli from UCSB."

"Yes, I am, and I do have one more school to visit and that is located in Morro Bay. I will go look at it and come back." We agreed that I would come back after I saw the school in Morro Bay, but I never came back to Cambria. Morro Bay was an elementary school and middle school combined. It was a beautiful coastal town with the school built in Spanish-style architecture with a bell tower. I went in. No one was in the office. I heard someone working in the nurse's room. A man on a stepladder was painting the walls white.

"I'm looking for the principal."

He looked down at me. "Are you Mr. Korisheli?"

I was stunned. "Yes, I am, sir."

"Well, I'm the principal." That settled my indecision. I would take this job if he offered it to me. We went for lunch and had a good interview. "Come the day after tomorrow and I'll have the board interview you. Good luck."

In two days, I was in front of the board of Morro Bay school, first through ninth grade system. I was impressed with their straightforward questions.

"You are stepping into big shoes, Mr. Korisheli," Mr. Patrick Nagano, one of the board members told me. I liked his direct, straightforward statement. After they came to the end of the inquiry, they said, "Now do you have some questions?"

"Yes, I do. I would like to know if I could have some time in the lower grade classrooms for ear training and music reading, beside the orchestra and the band instrumental groups." I noticed a little pause and guessed that they hadn't had that before.

One of them said, "We will discuss it and let you know our decision."

The next day I went to the principal's office.

"Yes, all is well. You are hired. Let me take you out for lunch again." Here again I picked up a friend, Mr. Wilmer Tognazzini. I was excited to work hard, but things did not go too well. I had a strong 70-piece band, well-trained for shows and marching. When I put the new music in front of them, I picked a very easy number to see how they would sight-read. They could not play at all.

It was a disaster. I could not figure it out. I stopped the group and finally asked, "What is wrong?"

Finally one student raised his hand. "We have to write the fingerings over the notes."

Well, I was facing very raw material. I did not give in. Within three months, the big group of 70 students went down to two dozens students. They were quitting.

The picture did not look very rosy. I went to my friend the principal to tell him that I would finish the year and then I would move on somewhere else. He didn't quite see such a dark future because the lower grades were doing very well in ear training and reading music. Here is what happened: by the end of the year, about twenty students who stayed with me did a very, very fine end-of-the-year spring concert. They played beautifully and the place was packed with parents who were curious about my resignation. The students presented a fine, carefully polished performance. I had the string groups playing and marching in the auditorium and finishing the performance on the stage — a very well-played number. The small band sounded great and on top of all that, I had the students sight-read a piece they had never seen before. The audience was great and I did not announce my resignation. The board member, Mr. Nagano, approached me and told me I should stay.

Things went so great that my principal gave me a separate building at the back of the school which became a little music conservatory. I started rehearsals and individual help every morning at 7 a.m. — one hour before the school bell would ring. Parents were my best assistants. Kids were on time without fail. The population of Morro Bay was not much over 5,000. One-fourth of the population was fishermen, and their children were always early arrivers. Another fourth were small business owners, and they were great organizers. The rest were early-retired citizens and farmers with fewer children, so I had everything I needed to build up some good sounds. There was no limitation to financing my orders of music or instruments. Morro Bay was not incorporated and the large PG&E power plant was putting lots of money into education.

One of the school board members, Mr. Adams, was a realtor. I had his child in my music class, and she was doing quite well. During the parent-teacher conference, I told him that his child was very talented. He tried to persuade me to purchase a piece of land.

"You'll be with us from now on. I am offering you a very good deal: a lot on a street with nothing but pine trees on Piney Way." He was very persuasive, and the price was low enough for a beginning teacher's salary. I agreed to see the lot. I had never owned any piece of property, and when I stepped on the beautiful grass and forest of pine trees, the aroma reminded me of ambrosia, and I decided to settle myself in Morro Bay. I bought the lot — the old saying goes that man is drawn to the earth. That was coming true.

I spent the weekends grooming the trees and some volunteer wildflowers. Next to my lot, a middle-aged couple was building a small house — a cabin. The wall on my side was unfinished and open. Seeing me working next door, they started inviting me for lunch.

"We are going to be neighbors," they told me. I started to dream of building a music studio.

"I would love to be your neighbor," I replied and started to enjoy them very much.

School kept me busy, but some days I was on my property. Mr. and Mrs. Mahr were finishing the open wall. They called me for lunch, and I noticed that they did not have the same jovial friendly faces.

"Is there something wrong?" I asked.

"Yes, there is. We will not be neighbors after all." Then they explained to me that Mr. Mahr did not get the job at the county office, and they had to keep their old house in Barstow. I told them how sorry I was and asked if I could do something to help.

"Yes, you can. We talked last night and we want you to finish our unfinished house. That would make us happy."

"But I just bought this lot and this is my first teaching job."

"You have that nice little Volkswagen Bug. Why don't you ask the bank if they would give you a loan on it." After much debate and convincing me that I couldn't go wrong, I went to the bank. They gave me $750. When I told Mr. Mahr about the bank's offer he said that was exactly 10% of the price, and the materials were there for the finishing touches. We went to the bank. After all the negotiations, I became the owner of the house and the adjacent lot. My colleagues at school were encouraging me to finish and move in. They started to give me a hand and help on weekends. I moved in, and in accordance with our Georgian tradition, I invited the whole school for the house-warming. It was a great party, just like in Georgia. My father was smiling up there!

I fell in love with my house. It was all wooden and had a very warm, inviting atmosphere. It had a large space in the back yard. I started to plan for the music studio and started reading literature about music buildings and acoustics and how to achieve a good sound. Finally I drew a simple plan.

The small fishing town of Morro Bay did not have very strict architectural requirements in 1957. All I had to draw was the floor plan with a sufficient number of windows, sewer and the location in relation to the street. The plan was to put the music studio in the backyard. I got my permit without any questions. My problem was the huge pile of redwood Mr. Mahr left in my backyard: beautifully selected boards, nicely stacked with spaces to ventilate the boards so they wouldn't gather mold. I finally called Barstow and got Mr. Mahr on the phone.

"The wood pile you left in the back yard — when are you going to take it?"

"What wood pile, Botso? That wood pile is yours; it was part of the deal. It's all yours." Then he told me how his father's lumberyard in Barstow went into bankruptcy and they hauled all the select lumber to Morro Bay for their house. I was now more than ready to go ahead with my studio plan. In one of the books I read about the importance of the room to have height, but with an interruption of some mezzanine-type of floor. I used to like A-frame wooden houses, and then I had an idea to put the "A" upside down and then the middle of the letter "A" would become the mezzanine, supported with some extension of the beams which gave stability to the inverted "A". The idea was pretty good, I thought. Now, I never studied building technique or architecture. Neither did my dad, but when he decided to build our family's dream house to move us from our small little place, he did the same thing. He would go to the new place and work together with house builders. He designed lots of things himself, and I was always by his side. I must have unknowingly adopted some abilities to develop a vision and a sense of construction and design. I was struggling with stress regulations, however. Here came another star in my life. Two houses from me was a very attractive wooden building, also redwood. I used to walk around that house and study how the studs were joined. Mr. Berghell, the house owner, who turned out to be an architect and a retired physics teacher from USC, noticed my curiosity.

"What are you building, my neighbor, if I may ask you?"

I was happy that he noticed me and wanted to talk to me. "A music studio, sir."

He wanted to know what I was studying about his house. I explained everything I learned in my readings, and I also told him how I liked his building.

"Let us go over and you can show it to me." He expressed eager interest. "Are you a musician?" I told him my ambitions and that I was a pianist and teaching music in the local school. My ambition was to build a studio to continue to pick up my musical career. He started to come every weekend when I worked. Another great friend. As we got to know each other, he showed me the letters from Jan Sibelius who was in correspondence with him. It was exciting to read the great composer's letters which were so beautifully humble and appreciative of Berghell's admiration. Berghell loved music, which was the beginning of our friendship.

He corrected my mistakes and adjustments. I had my inverted "A" frame ribs tied together, just to keep them up. He did something very interesting: he dowelled each rib into the cement with metal dowels. This was intended to withstand the vertical and horizontal earthquake shocks. The inspector had to be called to inspect the building. When he came, he looked at it and said, "No, sir, I'm not going to sign the permit for this. I won't even go inside the building. I wouldn't trust it."

That was bad news. I went to Mr. Berghell and told him what the inspector said.

"Let me call the county chief architect and see what is going on." Berghell's name was well-known to architects. I found out that my friend was also an advisor of British ship building which was the most famous in the world. The architect knew that also. The architect came and saw what Mr. Berghell was trying to do to withstand the strongest earthquakes by dowelling the ribs into the cement. After an explanation, the architect was very impressed. He particularly praised the connections of the foundation to the frame ribs. Mr. Berghell made me pin every bottom of the frame with vertical bolts.

Getting involved in architecture, I met a very talented young professor at Cal Poly, Ron Morgan. After I told him the story of my studio, he was interested to see it. He told me that he was most impressed by the human dimensions I used to build the entire construction. And he asked if he could bring his seminar to lecture inside my music building, which he did. It was quite beneficial both ways.

Now I was completing the studio and could hardly wait to try the acoustics and start some recitals and traditional house concerts. I finally asked my friend, a violinist named Stanley Plummer to initiate the studio and try out the acoustics. Stanley just finished his debut at Carnegie Hall and was leading the string department at UCLA — a fine violinist. It was wonderful to dedicate the studio with unaccompanied Bach, which was the entire program. The acoustics turned out great and I was happy. Bach was always my ideal. Mr. Berghell's suggestions for designing and extending the mezzanine for the sound interruption turned out very well. The studio became a place for performances.

The city of San Luis Obispo was attracting some very fine musicians. I suggested having the old traditional house concerts with the brass-choir overture performances as an introduction. The idea was very welcomed by musicians and by the audience. I was able to entice my Santa Barbara musician friends. My former string instructor at UCSB, Stefan Krayk, became my concertmaster and Cliff Swanson, who was creating an instrumental music department at Cal Poly, joined me and brought some string players with him. We managed to have two or three concerts per year, which brought lots of joy. I was able to establish a certain kind of tradition — no politics, no publicity and no financial involvement whatsoever. It was free to be enjoyed. That still prevails until today.

Although things were going well at my work, something was missing. At UCSB I met a fine musician, Patricia Smith, who also volunteered to be my usherette at my senior recital. After we got to know each other, we decided to put our lives together in 1958. We worked a system where she would prepare young piano students for me and I'd continue for further training on the keyboard. After six years we adopted our son, Temmo, and two years later our daughter, Tina. (I was happy with my family until Patricia decided to leave us to have a different kind of life. I had to go through some difficult years raising two teenage children. They became beacons of my life. After they finished their education, Temmo chose to be a musicologist and followed my footsteps, and Tina majored in anthropology. My two children flew out of the house and I was again alone for a while.)

Through UCSB I was introduced to Dr. Erik Katz from New York School of Music. Erik, a musicologist from the University of Freiburg, was deeply involved in Renaissance and early Baroque music. He got me interested in it and asked me to start a group here in Morro Bay. Dr. Katz already had a very strong music collegium in Santa Barbara playing viola da gambas, recorders and all early Baroque and late Renaissance instruments. I found some enthusiasts in Morro Bay and was able to create an attractive group. Erik kept coming with his group, and we managed to convert the studio into the sounds of 16th- and 17th-century music. Dr. Katz decided to unite the northern collegium with the south and asked me since Morro Bay was in the middle between San Francisco and Los Angeles, why not get the group together in Morro Bay. We did. There were about 30 musicians creating authentic Renaissance music with the viola da gambas, the recorders, crumhorns, the small percussion, all concertizing under the direction of Dr. Katz.

After Stalin's death in 1953, the Iron Curtain restrictions were considerably reduced and closer to 1960 the cultural exchanges started to appear. That was the year I heard from Mother. Thanks to Mr. Ed Sullivan who negotiated the cultural exchanges with the Soviet Union, the Georgian Dance Troupe visited Los Angeles.

My friend Shota wrote to me that he had obtained tickets for the performance at the Shrine Auditorium. The huge place was packed beyond capacity. The performance was breath-taking. The American audience went into such an emotional excitement and the unbelievable leaps were greeted with loud applause. Vocal choruses accompanied the magnificent speed and footwork.

After the performance we decided to go to the stage entrance and see our countrymen. We found a KGB man guarding the door. I asked if we could see the dancers.

"What is your name?"

After I responded, I got a big surprise.

"There is a relative of yours and I'll tell him that you are here." How did he know that the dancer was my relative? That puzzled me for a long time.

We were admitted and one young fellow came to embrace me and I felt his hand in my coat pocket sliding something in. It was again a time of some change in my life. We spoke to each other for ten minutes. That was the limit I guessed. I went back to the KGB officer and asked him where they were staying.

"The hotel on Vine and Hollywood Boulevard."

"Can I come and see him again?"

After a little silence, he agreed.

"Come early in the morning."

I could hardly wait to check my pocket for the envelope he slipped in there. It was my mother's letter. It changed my life again. I felt like some heavy burden of clouds on my shoulder dropped off.

The letter said, "My son, this young man is our relative. He knew about our misfortunate life. When I heard that our dance company had engagements in different countries, I visited him and gave him this card. I told him, 'I know he must be alive and if you find him, I'll be happy for the rest of my life.' He was more than happy to look for you. I am in good health and thank heavens I can work. My hope is to receive some news about you, my son. You are my life torch. Mother."

I was determined to bring her to America. My efforts were encouraged by all my friends and all the officials I visited for consultations. Mother and I started to communicate. The letters were not very dependable, but some of them were reaching her.

Following the news of my intention to bring my mother to America, I met a young and very enthusiastic

TV news reporter. His named was Ed Porter. Somehow he heard of the news about my mother and I received a phone call.

"Hello, Mr. Korisheli? This is Ed Porter. Do you remember me? I am the news reporter on TV…Yes… We would like to have you over for a cup of coffee this evening. I think you will be very happy about what I have to say to you. It concerns your mother. Can you make it?... Fine. We'll see you shortly."

When I arrived, Ed was very excited. He introduced me to his wife Ruth and offered me a comfortable chair. He was young, but his serious expression made him look older. When Ed started to explain the plans about my mother, my face appeared happy, but not as he expected. I listened carefully to the entire story with a pleasant and controlled smile. He told me how he was going to make sensational news about mother. He also told me how he inquired about the possibilities of bringing my mother to the USA. When Ed finished, there was a silence. I didn't answer immediately. That surprised the couple.

Finally, I put my coffee down and with the same smile said, "I'm sorry, Mr. Porter, but I don't think my mother nor I will be happy with such a plan."

Ed was quiet.

"But Mr. Korisheli. I am serious," he said.

I wasn't smiling any more. I spoke in a low, convincing voice. "Your intentions are most kind indeed, Mr. Porter, but you have to understand. You see, I am the only son, and this news means an awful lot to her. I don't think she will be happy if her feelings will be exposed to the public." I stopped and looked at Ruth. "These feelings are so dear to us, that we would like to keep them as our very own."

"Do you intend to bring her over here sometime?" asked Ruth.

"Yes, I would like to save money and bring her for a short visit to start with and if I can, I'll keep her with me."

"Speaking of money, I forgot to mention that the network will pay for all expenses," said Ed loudly.

"No, Mr. Porter. Again you must understand. If I bring her here, I will do it with my own money."

There was a long silence. Ruth's eyes grew sad. I guessed her thoughts. She wondered how she would feel if she lost her boy for twenty years, and she looked straight into my eyes.

Ed lit another cigarette, poured some more coffee and said, "I'm sorry, but I don't understand you. Most families would be proud to be on TV. I just don't understand it." He sounded disappointed.

Ruth felt uncomfortable when she noticed my face. I was looking at her as if to tell her, "I appreciate so much your husband's efforts. I don't like to disappoint him." Ruth knew that Ed never would understand. She tried to change the conversation.

"Can I get you a piece of pie, Mr. Korisheli?" she asked.

"No thank you. I must be going home soon."

"How about some more coffee?" she tried to persuade me.

"No thank you. I really must be going."

I arose, shook Ed's hand and said, "I'm sorry, Mr. Porter. I hope this case won't create any unpleasantness with your work."

"Oh, no. That's OK. You sure you won't change your mind?"

I shook my head and with a laugh added, "I won't." I offered my hand to Ruth and squeezed it tightly. "Thank you for the coffee."

"I'll take you out to your car," said Ed. He walked with me out the front door while Ruth remained in the doorway. She watched me get in my car and drive off.

In a year, I had all the necessary documents to bring Mom to me. Then came the devastating news. The excitement about finding me was too much of an emotional shock. She had a breakdown and never recovered. I never heard the details of her departure.

When the news arrived, I did not want to believe it. For a few moments I was frozen. Then I went out in the yard and started splitting and chopping logs wildly. I must have been doing this for many hours until I was completely exhausted, fell down on the ground and sobbed.

The memories of my time with Mother are with me for the rest of my life. One thing did comfort me and kept her presence with me. When we were parting she said, "If something should happen to me, I want you to watch butterflies. When one comes close to you, that one is me." It is strange how this beautiful image and gorgeous creatures make me happy, particularly when they get very close to me.

My dream was to create a county youth symphony. I was still determined to enlarge the musical culture among the young people. In 1961, I started to ask the local county music teachers for string players. The only few string groups were in Pismo Beach Junior High with Mr. Marion Mureno and San Luis Obispo High School with Lucian Morrison. They sent string players to my studio, plus my own students. We started practicing once a week as a small group. Thanks to the county music teachers, I was able to grow the group into a full-sounding orchestra. The studio was not large enough and again the teachers' help was a God-send. Mr. Blakeslee from Cuesta College, Mr. Stubson at San Luis Obispo High and, later, Mr. Sando at Laguna Junior High all were generous in sharing their practice facilities with us. Teachers would help me to audition students for the orchestra. Within four years, we were able to give three concerts each year. We started summer camps and exchanged concerts with Santa Barbara Youth Symphony, Laguna Beach, Monterey Bay Youth Symphony and we started traveling and were invited to give performances up north at Foothill College and De Anza College and to the south at Santa Barbara and San Diego high schools.

Around this same time I was building up the San Luis Youth Symphony, I followed my talented elementary school orchestra over to Morro Bay High while continuing at Morro Elementary School. My student, January Munro Anderson, recalled this time in a letter to the Telegram Tribune, our local newspaper:

"There are no shortcuts! You must practice!"

Botso Korisheli used to tell that to us daily, starting when we were only six and seven years old. We were the first generation of his orchestra students in Morro Bay. When we left our elementary school in the late '60s for the Junior-Senior High School, he switched teaching jobs and went with us, and our remarkable little award-winning string orchestra toured the state almost every year until we graduated.

Also my piano teacher, Mr. Korisheli miraculously charmed me into practicing up to three hours a day; thus I knew the indescribable joy of exploring Bach's brilliant two-part inventions, hours on end. And on my violin, I let my soul sing and cry; Mr. Korisheli taught me how.

I don't play piano at all any more, and only play my violin as secret therapy. But Mr. Korisheli's influence, staunchly given with love and a rare respect for dignity, was profound far beyond music.

For he only taught me the truth- a most glorious, beautiful truth: There are no shortcuts.

My students have heard me say that to exist, to be creative and to pay your dues to the world, you need five things: family, friends, music, work, and love. Students were becoming part of my life, giving me feelings of belonging to a large family. All five things I inherited from my parents and grandparents and were deeply instilled in my system.

I was assigned to Morro Bay High School to build up the music, Latin and humanities programs. My string program was in great shape. I had wonderful students for all my classes and I was inspired. All was going well except for one thing. I was never instructed nor trained for parade shows with a marching band. Being a pianist and focused on the orchestra, I was lost when the request came to have a half-time show for the football game and a marching unit for city events.

At the conservatory of music, marching bands were never mentioned and at UCSB music department I never had a course in marching bands, so I was in the dark. How should I solve the problem? After trying to put some drums and trumpet fanfares together for the games, I realized that they were all right, but they didn't excite the crowd. Then I decided to do something sensational, something like the Romans would do when the gladiator was fighting the lion.

I decided to build a giant bass drum. I sketched out a drum with a six-foot diameter and two feet deep. I should be made of stainless metal with a thin fiber head stretched over it and painted with a portrait of a pirate with a knife in his mouth (the Morro Bay High School mascot.) Then I designed a four-wheel trailer to be pulled by four men.

I presented the sketch to our metal shop teacher, Sam Boyd, who was also the football coach. He was more excited than I was and even shouted "Hurrah!" We raised the money and built the drum. The result was a sensational sight. We rolled out the show with the four men dressed as Roman slaves (and representing the visiting team) and the two girls in their pirate uniforms with huge mallets hitting the drum on each side. The crowd went wild. It turned out to be a great presentation and I was saved.

The passage of Proposition 13 in 1978 slowed down and almost eliminated orchestral education in public schools, but in Morro Bay we managed to keep the High School string orchestra for a little longer. Some music teachers from Santa Barbara and San Diego had asked me to bring the string orchestra to encourage their administrations to reinstate their orchestras, which we enjoyed very much. I would like to express my deepest gratitude to the Kronos Quartet for helping my string program in the early 1980s by giving us free clinics and inspiring demonstrations. They opened up incredible possibilities of creating magical sounds on strings and embedded a permanent appreciation for musical culture in our lives.

Even with such prominent outside help, it was not possible to continue the string program in the schools under Proposition 13, but I was determined to keep the instruction in the lower grades, where it was not classified as an "orchestra." The new schedules allowed us to do some work in the lower grades under the title "Music Education in the Classrooms."

No budget for instruments was available. Having a good results in 2nd and 3rd grades with the string instruments, my mind was made up. I was going to do something to have some feeder instruments for the upper grades. I decided to make a small violin-shaped string instrument. I cut 2 x 6 pine wood into ½ and ¾ sized violins. I purchased piano strings and strung up two pitches, A and E. For the bow, I ordered 30 half-sized bows from China. The Chinese instruments were not expensive and the bows were only one dollar.

I prepared myself for a bold step and went to my principal and asked if I could use some kind of instruments that would give me an accurate pitch to train the students. I explained to him that I would be able to accomplish three things: ear-training, reading of music, and being ready to play musical instruments. He was very supportive for the program as long as there was no financial commitment for the future.

I needed help. In our middle school we had a wonderful woodshop teacher, Mr. Kent Wetzel. I showed my 2 x 6 pine violin to him, and he got very excited. "That is a great program for my class," he exclaimed.

In less than two weeks I had 30 violins made of pine wood with two strings. I was able to teach "Hot Cross Buns" and in less than two months, kids were able to play the famous "Twinkle, Twinkle, Little Star" with fairly accurate pitches.

Classroom teachers were more than happy to bring the class to the cafeteria where I used to have the instrumental groups. Children were very enthused to put the 2 x 6 violins under their chins (I padded the chins with some donated foam rubber.) For the next Christmas program, I had them play an enchanting concert. All was legal, my principal told me. Everyone was happy, thanks to our woodshop teacher, our classroom teachers, wonderful parents and our principal.

Here is a rough sketch of my 2 x 6 violin:

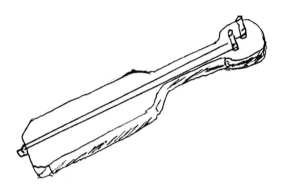

For the Youth Symphony we started summer camps. A fine violinist named Carol Kersten joined me to coach the strings, which was a great help.

Aside from my teaching duties at Morro Elementary and Morro Bay High School, I needed some of my very own spiritual activities. My dad and I used to hike a lot. I realized that my spiritual commitments were very closely connected with the nature. Every time we had a vacation, Dad and I would hike. Sometimes we spent a whole week hiking in the mountains. I often expressed to my friends the wish for them to hike with me. I found a friend in my classroom in my junior year in Georgia, and the wonderful memories are still with me.

In my class I had a friend who was from the Georgian region of Svanetia, Dzuria Djaparidze. I expressed to him how much I missed hiking with my father. "Would you like to spend a summer with me?" he approached me.

Dzuria and I became very close friends. I started to spend summers with him in his homeland. The snow-covered peaks where Prometheus had been chained. Cold fast streams where shepherds stored the sheep's fleeces under the rocks to trap the gold flakes, the "golden fleece" which had attracted Jason with his Argonauts.

We played, we hiked, we picked some wild fruits and flowers. I still enjoy remembering the times. Now, in Morro Bay without my dad, I missed the connection with our mother earth. There must be some metaphysical solutions in our desires.

A teacher moved into our area — Dick Rush. He took the teaching position at Cambria High School, in my neighboring town. I met him through his future wife, a very accomplished musician, and with my wife Patricia we created a fine quartet of Renaissance recorder music. One glorious thing was that Dick was an unstoppable hiker. Long miles, difficult trails, steep mountains — rain or shine would not stop us from hiking.

CHAPTER FIVE:

VENTANA HIKES

"Nature that fram'd us of four elements,
Warring within our breasts for regiment,
Doth teach us all to have aspiring minds."
Christopher Marlowe, *Conquests of Tamburlaine*, Part I

To cross the Ventana Wilderness from Big Sur to the San Antonio Mission takes three nights and four days. Crossing these 80 miles was like the experience of going through life one more time. There is a folklore belief that we humans change and grow in different stages of our lives every seven years. During the fall hikes, we plowed through the dead, dry leaves. It was an unforgettable sound, telling us we had not given up. We give the warm blanket to mother earth to keep her going to the next year. What memorable conversations we cherished with nature. We came to a river bed once which was washed naked with the storm water. Somehow in the middle, a young willow survived, standing up straight all alone, missing the family. Then something strange happened. Dick was crossing the dry bed to see if there was another trail on the other side. I stayed behind watching him. He walked close to the willow and I saw the plant slowly leaning toward him.

"Watch the plant, Dick! Go on the other side." He did, and the plant slowly leaned toward him again. The poor young plant, the poor young child, was looking for warmth. That was a dramatic picture. I often wonder what happened to our lonely friend, did he survive? Or was he washed out?

I remember my father's favorite poem. In Georgia, we have a legend about Mindia. a man who loved nature more than anything. He was able to converse with trees and flowers and animals. He could understand their language. The legend goes that Mindia ate snake meat and that enabled him to understand nature's language. Here is the poem by our poet, Vazha Pshavela.

Flowers with their tilted necks.
Attractive, beautiful as ink drawings.
In unison they murmur, a tender sound.
"Hail to you, Mindia. Take me. Carry me."
Mindia plucks them lovingly.
Greets the morning mist tenderly.
Another day Mindia goes to cut the tree.
Swinging his axe, he hears the sigh,
"Don't cut me, my friend Mindia. Don't take my sunlight soon away.
You are armed and I am not. Spare me. Spare me, Mindia."
Mindia's arms drop down shamefully,
Turning to the next tree, swinging the axe,
Heart-breaking pleading stops him again.

My father used to portray Vazha Pshavela in one of the dramas written for the stage. He was very highly acclaimed for reciting poems. He memorized most of his poems. The poem about Mindia was my favorite, and I memorized them also. On my hike, I used to catch myself reciting them silently.

The first camp where we used to spend the night was Sikes, the Southfork River. The river worked some wonders widening the canyon and made the most luscious place to camp. On top of all this beauty, there was a sulfur bath there. You could sit in it and forget about the high-tech spas with all types of jets and lights and paraphernalia. Sikes' natural holes in the ground were the best spas I have ever experienced. Sulfur minerals made us feel like newborns again. The next camp on the route to San Antonio Mission was the Redwoods. According to our forest ranger, who often would catch up with us on his horseback, the redwoods were receding toward the north. A few centuries ago, they were quite prolific, as far south as San Diego. Camp Redwood was a distinguished place now. We never stayed there — just a snack and then we went on to the Rainbow. That camp was where Dick would catch trout. It was great to have a friend who had a secret, laconic language with fish. They would listen to him, but they would never listen to my painful persuasion to get close to my bait.

Once, I remember in our Sierra hikes, we were getting low on food. We were above timberline. The lake looked isolated and deserted. "I hope there will be some fish here," I exclaimed. In less than one hour, Dick caught four fish. I started the fire and we did not wait for the other side of the fish to be cooked. We started eating the cooked side right off the grill. At the Rainbow camp, we had fish as usual. The hike and crossing the wilderness was hard physically and psychologically. Each camp was on the bottom of the hill. To get to the next camp, the trail goes up and down, sometimes fairly steep mountains. On one hike, Dick's friend was eager to join us. As the hike got harder and harder, and more difficult, her questions mounted.

"How much more? How much more?"

I acquired a trail psychology somewhere, maybe from my father. I would say, "It will be this steep hill and then the next will be easier." Nothing was getting easier. In the end, she finished the hike, but I think we lost a friend.

We never heard a word from her again.

Once we tried another friend. I met someone in Santa Barbara who was admiring the type of hikes we were doing.

"Can I go with you sometime?" he pleaded. Dennis was his name. He came to Morro Bay with equipment that would have impressed Himalayan mountaineers. We had everything. As we got closer to half-way, Dennis was getting tense. There were some rattlesnakes on the trail and that made him nervous. At the rest place, he opened his knapsack and we saw a handgun. He was putting it in the front pocket for easy accessibility. I suppose he was going to use it on snakes. That was against our style and our hiking philosophy.

We decided to cut the hike short by leaving the trail, going cross-country. We both had a good sense of orientation, aiming toward the coast to pick up Highway One and hike to our car. He was convinced that we were getting lost, and he got shaky and scared. We managed to get closer to the ridge and, lucky us, there was a commune of monks, called Camaldolese, an independent, hermetic order, living a solitary life and defying the forms of ordinary life. We found a shady place and lay down our hiker. He had a physical breakdown. We tried to get someone to look after him while we went down to the highway and hiked to our truck. Nothing moved. Nobody came out. We knew they would not come out and leave their solitude that particular day. We got some water close to Dennis and told him to stay there until we got back. We left, and we were lucky to hitchhike about twenty miles to our truck in Big Sur. When we came back, Dennis was still lying on the ground. I think the monks were watching from a distance, but they never came close to him. There was no contact with the other world, except one day of the week when they opened the gates and people could visit, but this was not that day of the week.

We put Dennis in the truck and drove home. He recovered enough to drive back to Santa Barbara. We never saw him again. The best news we received two years later was that Dennis was educating people for hikes. He became a Sierra Club member and was organizing some hikes himself. With quiet smiles we both felt good about that and were waiting to hear similar news from Dick's old girlfriend, we hoped.

The next camp, Mocho, was just to catch the breath. The Mocho camp was a spring-board toward our last part of the hike, to Lost Valley. It was a small camp, but its one advantage was that if you had to cut the hike short, there was a trail going up to the ridge and it was one way to get back to your car in Big Sur. I remember once we decided to cut our hike short and did take that trail to the ridge to get back to camp. Something very strange happened to us. At one part of the trail it was quite steep and had sharp slopes on both sides. We were about halfway up and we heard some crashing noise. A wild boar was looking at us. We were about twenty feet apart. We stood there for a long time. We tried to guess his thoughts and he was trying to guess ours, I think. He did not move. We finally figured out his thinking. His reasoning was that he couldn't go up the steep hills or go down. He would roll down and it would be disastrous for him. We agreed with his thinking and started to climb up the hill to the closest tree and give him the right-of-way. We sat there for quite some time. Finally, he realized that he had the free way, and then he slowly descended. People say that pigs are more intelligent than dogs. That may be right. We went our way and he went his way. All was good.

After Mocho camp, we were getting into the luscious last part of the hike called Lost Valley, properly named because the waters were disappearing into the valley and of course, the green vegetation was just beautiful and luscious. We rarely stopped at the Tan Oaks, a small camp, but we did enjoy the Pilon, that's almost the last camp. Sometimes we stayed there because there was such a lovely pool. We'd get inside the pool and glorify our hikes. The next day, going to the seventh camp, named Fish Camp, we walked out to the roads built for machines where our wives would be waiting to take us home. What a feeling of accomplishment and elevation of being part of our mother earth.

CHAPTER SIX:

GEORGE

"You are in need and troubled?
Put your arm over my shoulder;
I'll walk with you."
Platon Korisheli

I always worked around the house on my weekends. Although I stayed away from publicity, somehow the story of my music studio building got in the coastal small-town paper. The article was short and nicely written, so it did not offend me. In fact, it led to one of the most important changes in my life. There are not many Georgian immigrants in America, especially at that time — not more than a few hundred. We have certain habits, to live like eagles — seldom in colonies. In the neighboring town of Cambria, about 12 miles from Morro Bay, there turned out to be one more Georgian immigrant, George Papashvily and his American wife, Helen. George was a well-known sculptor and Helen was a highly-respected writer. Helen read the town newspaper with my name and the story about my music studio. She showed it to George, telling him that there was another Georgian in the neighboring town. George's reply was, "Oh no, there are no other Georgians around here." Then Helen showed him my name — Wachtang — there is no other nation in the world who would use that Georgian name. George had to give in, and they decided to look me up.

As usual, I was working around the house when an elderly man with a large moustache walked up to the house and shouted, "Kartveli khar?" which in Georgian means, "Are you Georgian?" I dropped my hammer. I could not believe my eyes and my ears.

"Kartveli var!" I shouted back. "Yes, I am Georgian." I ran down toward him. We hugged like father and son. I felt like the world was telling me something. "Sit down, my son," the world said. "You are going to have a good life."

George and Helen became part of my family. He had a large house and sculpting studio in Quakertown in Pennsylvania, and a small studio in Cambria. In winter, when he could not sculpt in Pennsylvania because of the weather and snow, they would come to California. And lucky me, they chose Cambria!

The weekends with the Papashvilys became a tradition. We never used the house for our get-togethers. We packed a picnic and went where the stones and rocks were to be found — beaches, canyons, coves and anywhere where the stones were exposed. George started to train me in stone carving. The first year, he would not let me touch the hammer and chisel. I had to recognize the stones, and that was a very good lesson for me. Since the day he gave me the hammer and chisel and stone to carve, I have not stopped and never will stop until I can no longer lift the hammer. It was not only stone carving I learned from George, it was something we all need to learn and that is how to live simply and never falsify who you are, never pretend or try to be someone else. Some of the most unforgettable stories about his life became examples for me. Here is one I will never forget.

George used to drive all the way from Pennsylvania to California during the month of October. He had a motto on his license plate: "I brake for stones." Once he was passing highway construction near San Diego, he noticed a large stone in the field and he stopped the car to check it with the geological hammer that he carried with him all the time. The stone turned out to be a good one, but too heavy to get into the car, so George chiseled his initials on the large stone "GP" — as he always did. A year later, he was driving the same highway coming to California and stopped to see his stone (he had a remarkable memory). Helen stayed in the car and George went to the field to check his stone. The stone was there, but it had been turned over. In the meantime, the Highway Patrol pulled up and asked Helen what was going on. The sign on the freeway said "No stopping at any time." Helen pointed to George and said, "Ask him."

The two tall policemen approached George slowly. "Sir, you should not be handling anything here and you should not stop the car on the freeway."

"What do you mean I shouldn't touch anything? This stone belongs to me." The policemen looked at each other. "Don't just stand there. Turn it over and you'll see my name."

This time the big fellow spoke, "Let us do it."

On the other side of the rock in big letters said "GP".

"This is a beautiful rock and it will be sculpted."

The policemen were attentively quiet.

"Don't just stand there. Help me put it in my car so I can move it."

Well, George got his stone in his car and the two policemen waved at him as he drove off. That was George. An unforgettable man who taught me so much.

My sculpting became my second discipline. After teaching many hours, I craved physical work which was given to me by the hammer and chisel and stones. George asked me to work one summer in his Pennsylvania studio. Again I picked up so much from his relationship with nature. George could barely read or write, but the University of Pennsylvania gave him an honorary doctorate for his keen power of observation and his dedication to nature and living things. His nine acres were in the most beautiful part of Pennsylvania, called Bucks County. He named his farm Ertoba — in Georgian it means "togetherness." His love for animals was so great and dedicated that St. Francis would have been impressed. Consequently, the nine acres were heavily populated with deer, rabbits and all types of birds. The government approached him for some solutions. The neighbors were complaining, of course, because the animals would damage their gardens and vegetation. George willed his property to the government. In return, he asked for permission to put the sign "No Hunting" on his property. But something had to be done about the neighbors, so here is what the government suggested. They would put down a giant net for a short time and after the animals got used to it, they would lift the net with hundreds and thousands of rabbits with the helicopter and fly them to a place they could live without damaging crops. George had to agree to that and all was peaceful.

George's life was unique, exemplary and admirable. Pennsylvania University's art department made a documentary film about him. That inspired Helen to write the best-seller *Anything Can Happen* which became required reading for all high school seniors. It was filmed with José Ferrer portraying George. *Anything Can Happen* also became my favorite and I used to require it for my humanities class, and I used to get very impressive papers from the students. After I introduced Dick Rush to Helen and George, he became part of the whole family. The two of us became good ogres for George. When he found big stones, we had to pick them up and put them in his car. We were two very happy ogres.

When George was in his Pennsylvania studio, Dick and I kept the weekend rock hunt and picnic traditions very faithfully. Sometimes we included our students for discussions, good hamburger picnics and of course carrying the rocks to the cars. For a change, we were the masters and our senior students took the place of the ogres.

Once Dick was lecturing about the first pilgrim settlements in America. The talk included Plymouth Rock in Massachusetts where pilgrim separatists from the Church of England arrived on the Mayflower from

Plymouth, England. The rock became a historical symbol. One student asked, "How big is the rock Mr. Rush?" Dick tried to describe the size using his arms.

"It is not very big," Dick explained.

"Oh, don't tell Mr. Korisheli. He will make us drag it to his car."

"Don't worry," Dick said. "It is protected with a huge granite portico gate."

Tragedy is educational, according to Aristotle. In my opinion, by going through suffering and tragedy you learn to face them with feelings of survival — to live with the demands and powers of nature, to go on and finish what the others could not. My young years did teach me a lesson, losing my family. Now, in 1978, I lost George. We had to take him to the hospital. He was feeling weak and had pains. The diagnosis was pancreatic cancer. I was spending every weekend with him, hoping to see some improvement, but there was none. I thought that if I displayed some positive energy to encourage his self-motivation, it would help some. I took my brass ensemble from my orchestra and serenaded under his window at the hospital. He was happy and delighted, but the next day asked his doctor to come and see him and talk. Dr. Morgan was a very wonderful person who also loved George.

When Dr. Morgan came for a straight talk, George said, "Tell me, doctor. Can you cure me?"

There was dead silence for a while.

Then Dr. Morgan said, "George, if you had any other part of the body with cancer, I would operate, but the condition of your pancreatic cancer is inoperable." The same evening, George asked me to take him home and the next morning Helen's sobbing message on the phone was that he had passed away. I think he knew that he was going to die and wanted to be at home.

We cremated him. Helen took his ashes to Quakertown and spread half of them across his beautiful grounds. The same summer she asked me to come and help her. It was not an easy job for me to clean up the sculpting studio. Helen picked up a granite slab from George's stone piles and asked me to put it behind the stone with the inscription, "So many more to come." I completed the work, and she put the other half of the remaining ashes in front of the stone, and I came back to Morro Bay.

"So many more to come." What a tribute, love, and respect for humanity. 'Take my place — I had a good life, and now it is your turn,' George was saying. For me, my wish is to teach my children and my students that death is part of us, part of the nature we live in.

My teaching commitments were increasing and my piano practicing for performances was decreasing. I had to make up my mind about not worrying about my recitals and spend my energy on my students. I also noticed that sculpting was starting to appeal to me more. I must have picked up some physical work habits in my lumberjacking years in the Bavarian Alps and my muscles were craving some activity. I had developed a strong habit for weekend sculpting. My adjacent lot was getting to look more and more like a sculpting yard. I started an impressive rock library thanks to my senior students with their great ability and willingness to carry heavy stones for me.

In my Freiburger years I enjoyed playing outdoor chess not far from the university. Once I happened to play a game with a fellow who told me that he carved the chess figures out of wood. A thought came to me: wouldn't it be wonderful to have an outdoor chess board in my own beautiful fishing town of Morro Bay? I drew the plans and presented them to the Morro Bay City Council. Luckily, one of the council members, Wayne Bickford, was very fond of chess and was a great wood carver. With his energy and enthusiasm, the plan was accepted.

We started to work together. The wood for the pieces came from two redwood water tanks which had served the city for 50 years. Two 6" x 12" redwood timbers were glued together and then cut and lathed into 22 inch pawns, 33 inch kings and 31 inch queens. The lathe was especially rigged for the job by Mr. Bickford. Members of the Morro Bay Chess Club also assisted with some of the labor of sanding and staining. The concrete chessboard was made up of alternate black and white 2 foot squares giving an overall dimension of 16 feet by 16 feet. Each chess piece weighed from 18 to 30 pounds. After the completion and the demonstration of the opening game, the city picked up good publicity in several major papers. It turned out to be the largest outdoor chess board in the country. The unveiling ceremony was filled with lots of joy.

Mr. Bickford suggested that I carve a memorial sculpture for Morro Bay. The city agreed to build a centennial staircase above my chessboard to connect the waterfront to the upper level of town for pedestrians. At that time the pelicans were becoming an endangered species according to biologists. This was caused by the deposits of DDT ending up in the ocean and weakening the strength of the pelicans' egg shells and not giving them enough time to hatch. I decided to sculpt a pelican family for the city.

In my activities I was also fortunate to befriend a local architect named James Maul. When I was telling him my idea he came up with a great suggestion.

"I have some good students in the Cal Poly architecture department. I'll be happy to let them design the centennial staircase and you can put your sculpture on the top landing which would give another attraction to the project." The City Council enthusiastically supported the project and I was able to select the boulder for the sculpture from among the boulders by Morro Rock.

The city became the motivating force for me to go all the way and create a professional sculpting studio. The council donated all kinds of materials for rock lifting including the I-beams with the powerful winch. They delivered stones and lumber for the chess carvings. We had the studio dedicated with Mayor Mitchell presiding.

CHAPTER SEVEN:

HOME

AND HOME AGAIN

Last of all we began the song of home,
"Georgia is a garden green–" our voices
rising over the walls, over the vines,
out to reach the stars.

George and Helen Papashvily, *Home and Home Again* (1973)

The village of Dimi in Georgia is my dreamland and will be all my life. Half of the population was related to each other historically. The name Korish was recorded in events when King Solomon in 1769, fighting the Turkish invaders, had a dear friend and dedicated fighter by the name Chikvinidze from the village Korish located on top of the mountains above the village of Dimi. Korish mountain village was a strategic point for King Solomon which became a historic location. Georgia went through a period when each province — east, south, north, west — had their own leaders and kings. Imereti and Korish were in the western part of Georgia. Visiting Georgia, one cannot help wondering how this little country withstood the invasions from so many sides. Muslim neighbors were determined to convert all the Christian countries to their religion. The main motivation was the fertile soil and the strategic points, plus the beauty of the nature.

Before the Muslims, Romans were drawn to Georgia for the same attraction. Roman generals believed Kolchis (which was the ancient name of Georgia) was a great strategic point. Touring Georgia, you will notice Christian churches surrounded with fortresses. Christianity was spread in fourth century, simultaneously with the Byzantine Empire and Constantinople. The archbishop Nestorius was the promoter of the expansion of faith, along with St. Nina. She was sent to Georgia with a cross made of wine twigs, and Georgia, being a cradle of wine culture, was thinking that the effort was well-timed, and the entire of Georgia accepted Christianity in a relatively short time.

My memories of Dimi are immortal. As a little boy, I was allowed to spend a part of the summer vacation with Grandma and Grandpa, who was a Georgian Orthodox priest. I loved the little corner with the wooden bed and its hay mattress. I loved the animals Grandma used to have around — the dog, Kursha, seemed to know the summer time when I was coming and always slept with me. We had one goat, one cow, seven chickens and one cat. I was put in charge of them and if you've never seen a happy caretaker, you should have seen me. I was in charge of getting the goat and cow ready at the gate for the shepherds who were collecting the village animals for grazing in the high meadows. I still dream about the herd of animals with the half-dozen shepherd dogs and shepherds with long walking sticks approaching our gate. The goat and cow did not have to be persuaded; they happily joined the blessed procession.

In the evening, the same parade would approach the village, and all I had to do was keep the gate open and the goat and the cow knew where to go, taking their respective places where I would milk them. The taste of the fresh milk is still on my lips. After almost 80 years, I keep the same habit by eating goat yogurt every morning and the memories hang around and linger so pleasantly.

I asked Grandma if I could go with the shepherds to spend the day. She was fine with that, except for one thing. My mother always insisted that I take a small, three-octave silent keyboard — I don't know where she found it. That keyboard, which I detested, did not have any sound and I had to practice for an hour each day. That hour was torture, but later on I found out something which has been so valuable for my teaching. That silent keyboard and one hour of torture taught me how to improvise. The sounds that I wasn't hearing, I was actually producing inside of me. Later on, my strongest point in my musical career was improvisation, thanks to that silent keyboard.

Grandma agreed that I could join the shepherds. I learned how to love nature. The fields were large and surrounded with small hills. One shepherd told me that right over the next hill was a herd of wild horses. I was dying to go there and watch them. After getting permission from Grandma and the shepherds, I started to spend a little time over the hill to watch the big family. I was in heaven seeing them play, run and graze. Once in a while I noticed they would glance at me and I would wave. Then I noticed a mother horse with a beautiful small colt near me. I plucked some tall grass and started to wave at them. I named the colt out of my own little fantasy, Rashi. In Georgian, Rashi was a legendary beautiful horse. I kept doing this every time I went with the shepherds, but the horses would not come to me. They would glance at me, but would not come close to me.

I loved being a shepherd. Grandma let me go with them in the morning hours. I had to be home for lunch to do some chores and for my practicing, of course. One day I noticed that the mother horse was coming a little closer to my fresh bunch of leaves, but would not get too close. The colt was always behind her. Then one day it happened. I was stretching my hand with long leaves and the colt came closer. I could hardly wait for the next day. I did the same thing and the colt was getting closer. The mother kept her distance and watched. I started calling, "Come Rashi, come." About the fifth day, she came and nibbled my grass bouquet. Again, I was floating in heaven.

Summer went fast and my parents and friends heard the story about Rashi more than a thousand times. Next summer came and Grandma was prepared for my shepherding activities. In the morning, I was with Rashi. She was shy at first, but I think she remembered me. After a week, she got in the habit of eating out of my hand and Grandma gave me some carrots under the one condition that I would not get my fingers too close to Rashi's lips because the teeth were quite sharp. "Open your palms when you give the food."

We made great friends. The third summer, Rashi was getting big and she would come and let me scratch her forehead. The next summer turned out to be a tragedy. My grandpa passed away and when I visited Grandma, she said some people came and rounded up all the horses and converted our small church into a stable. The Soviets used to just do that — to convert the churches for practical reasons. I went to the village church to see for myself what was going on. I loved that little church. We used to play hide-and-seek in the yard. My grandpa used to preach there. A wooden door was cut down like a horse stable and the floor was full of hay. The horses were against the wall. I took courage and plucked the weeds and called Rashi. She came to the gate. I was happy and I was crying. After I got home, Grandma tried to subdue my sobbing with hugs. Rashi had to be given up. Grandma moved in with us in Tbilisi, and we were happy to have her with us.

I never realized how close I was to my Grandma. One case showed me my attachment to her. She got into the habit of sitting in front of the fireplace, poking the ashes with the stick and repeating, "Come, Death, come. Do not prolong my life." That not only bothered me, but I was upset, alarmed, and worried. Something had to be done. One day my cousin Buta was visiting us. I told him my worries.

"What can we do to stop this habit?" I asked with an alarmed voice.

"I have an idea," he exclaimed. "When she gets to the fireplace and starts her murmuring, you go on top of the roof and shout down the chimney to scare her. I swear she'll never repeat that again. I'll watch for her and let you know when."

I went up on top of the roof next to the chimney, waiting for Buta to give me the sign when Grandma would start her pleas for Death to come for her. Buta came out and gave the sign, so I leaned over into the chimney and shouted down in my deepest, loudest voice — "I'm COMING!" Oh, my, she fell off her stool and shouted, "Help! Help!" and fainted. That was the end of her murmurings and was my first spanking. I was relieved of my worries and was happy when I was getting smacks. Grandma never asked Death to come again.

I also realized how much she loved me. One day she demanded to visit my school and sit in my class for the lecture. Now, that was not the usual practice for parents or grandparents to ask for permission to visit a class, but she had her persuasive and demanding way, so our director allowed her to come to the classroom for the day. I had an uneasy feeling at first, but after a while I was proud of her and my friends liked her very much.

Another time she got me in serious trouble. Grandma brought with her a beautiful icon and insisted it should hang in my room. Having my friends visiting me often, the word got out that Botso had an icon in his room. That was not smiled on by the Soviet system — for a young student to have an icon in the room. Word also got to the teachers and the school director. One day, I was called to the director's office. "Botso, I was told that you have an icon hanging in your room. You know it is not the proper thing to do. Why don't you take it down? Will you please?"

I hesitated for a while and then I said, "Yes, I will take it down if you talk to my grandma first."

A very quick response came back. "Oh, no, not the Grandma. That's OK."

That was the end of the icon case. No one complained or asked about it any more.

My most unforgettable event with Grandma was when she asked about my baptism and found out that I was not baptized.

"Why was Botso not baptized?" A stern-sounding question was put in front of my father.

"Mother, you know the rules of our system," Father was trying to say to her.

"System or no system. I want Botso to be baptized."

Here is what happened. Dad told his story to his stage director Akhmeteli.

"I don't see any problem," Director Akhmeteli said. "We have several actors who used to be priests. Let us set up a little stage in the theater and we will baptize

Botso. Be sure that Grandma gets here very early so that we don't have any witnesses and rumors getting around." It was done. Grandma and I were driven to the theater by horse buggy very early before the street guards got to work. In the theater, she was placed in the first row. The baptism was performed very successfully and she approved. I was delivered to the school and all was kept in tight secrecy.

In the evenings we developed a tradition of conversing about the events and happenings of the day. One unforgettable evening with Grandmother has stayed with me the rest of my life. Grandmother, knowing that religion was not practiced or talked about under the present regime, constantly reminded me that the Bible was written by the Holy Ghost. She also wished to know my parents' thoughts about the Trinity. She reiterated her belief in the Father, the Son, and the Holy Ghost, then turned to my mother and asked for her opinion. Mom was silent for a while and then said, "Grandma, to me it should be: 'Father/Mother;' 'Son/Daughter;' and 'miracles of nature.' We have the Trinity right here in our family."

There was another long silence and then she turned to my dad.

"And what do you think, son? What is in your Trinity?"

"Mother, I think we talked before when my father was alive. My Trinity is 'yesterday,' 'today,' and 'tomorrow.' In the first, I learn; in the second, I live, I work, and I pray. And the third is tomorrow, to which I look forward and eagerly anticipate." Dad was looking at me while talking to his mother. I knew what he had in mind: he was transferring his life-philosophy to me, and I inherited every word. I also live by my mother's humanistic logic and my grandmother's spirituality. I often catch myself reciting prayers which she so carefully instilled in me.

Many years later, when I was a student at UCSB, I heard an inspiring lecture about the Bible as literature by Professor Sturman. He was inviting questions and discussions. I told him the Trinity definitions in my family, and here is what he told me.

"You know, Bernard Shaw was asked whether he thought that the Bible was written by the Holy Ghost. His answer was, 'the Holy Ghost has not only written the Bible but all the good books in the world.'"

When I told him about my mom's opinion, he thought it was a great example of women's emancipation in the 20th century; and in response to my father's answer he told me to find the Sanskrit writing about saluting the dawn. I did find it, and quote it here:

"Salutation of the Dawn" (from the Sanskrit)

Listen to the Salutation of the Dawn.
Look to this day!
For it is life, the very life of life.
In its brief space are all the verities,
realities of your existence.
The bliss of growth,
The glory of action,
The splendor of beauty.

For yesterday is but a dream
And tomorrow only a vision,
But today well-lived makes
Every yesterday a dream of happiness,
And every tomorrow a vision of hope.
Look well therefore to this day.

Such is the Salutation of the Dawn.

CHAPTER EIGHT:

MARGARET

"God, the best maker of all marriages,
Combine your hearts in one."
William Shakespeare, *King Henry V*, ii

During the time while I was teaching in the public schools, giving house concerts, teaching private piano students, sculpting and hiking, my friend Lyle Porter, principal at a private Catholic school, and I would get together and discuss our teaching philosophy. Lyle was introduced to me when he was a counselor at our high school, and we found that we had the same teaching philosophy – education to knowledge, with a demanding approach. That was our priority. One day he told me that he hired an art teacher, Margaret Tarbell, who was anxious to sculpt stones. He described my activities and my commitment to art to her and introduced us. We started to work together. There is something unequalled — the relationship of carving stones together, two people create a piece that was never there before. We did just that. We created, not just sculpted, but we started to live together and got married in 1984.

I am convinced and believe that some guardian angels were looking after us. Could it be my mom, dad and grandma? My wish was to introduce Margaret to my country of Georgia. It was after perestroika in the USSR, and things were getting much safer for me to go back. We offered to Tbilisi, the capital of Georgia, a plan to do a tribute to the country by sculpting some public art. We were invited by the city and spent three months there to complete two sculptures for the historical part of the city. The reputations and status of my father and mother were reinstated, and we had a great welcome. My schoolmates were spoiling us. During the day we worked, and in the evenings they had parties for us. Seeing my classmates was rewarding. It was just like a family reunion. They had been on my side during the hard times, and now they welcomed us like brothers and sisters.

My brother Leo was not alive anymore, but his daughter (my niece) Nani and her family made me feel like I was coming home again.

The most exciting thing in my life was visiting Dimi — my grandparents' village on my father's side. On my mother's side, we lost parents too early and the stories about them were always second-hand.

I always shared all my memories with Margaret and we decided to take time out of our sculpting work and visit Dimi. It is a small village with not more than a hundred homes. Half of the villagers were Chikvinidzes and the other half Chkheidzes. They were primarily wine and vegetable growers. Chikvinidzes are our families. Father took 'Korisheli' as a stage-name for his acting career. Chikvinidzes were from the Korish mountain.

My grandparents' small house had been converted into a two-story house where my relatives live now. We had a wonderful reception, stayed two days and had a grand time. The most impressive event was when the head of the household performed the traditional wine urn opening ceremony. In Georgia, wine is kept cured in large, clay urns which are buried in the ground. The opening and tasting ceremony involves an impressive tradition. The host has to invite the oldest member of the village to get the first taste of the glass. The face of the elder taking the glass to her lips is watched with high tension by all. If the smacking lips and drinking a small gulp and if the eyes light up and the smile appears on the face, that was the beginning of the festivities. If she frowns, that means the host either had to go to the next urn or cover it up and open it up a year later. Well, here is what happened.

Everybody was quite tense when the host took out the first glass. Instead of giving it to the elder, he slowly handed it to Margaret. The wine was great and we had an unforgettable party. The next day, after we walked the village, every neighbor was trying to invite us to try their hospitality and try their wine. We could have stayed there longer, but the work was waiting for us in Tbilisi.

We said good-bye to beautiful Dimi and drove back to our work.

We finished our sculptures and the city gave us a wonderful dedication ceremony. It was 1991, the year of the coup d'état in Russia, and we almost did not get out of Moscow. All the flights were checked and eventually cancelled. With the connections of one relative, Temur Chkheidze, a drama director in Russia, we got onto the last plane before the cancellation. We brought with us my grand-niece, daughter of Temur, and she stayed with us a whole year. She went to the local private school where I taught, Mission College Prep in San Luis Obispo, and learned English quite well.

Hearing George's story, Margaret felt like she knew him. After we lost George, Helen was still keeping the tradition of coming to California in the winter months. Margaret and I spent some summer time with Helen in Quakertown. That summer, Helen wanted us to take some unfinished stones and wood and tools with us to Morro Bay. We had enough stones from Cambria, but we did decide to take the tree; that tree had some meaning and history for George's life. He grew the cherry tree, which eventually got old and had to be cut down. It was getting to the stage where it couldn't produce cherries anymore. He saved this huge big trunk. It was three feet in diameter and the piece we were looking at was eight feet long. We inherited this beautiful wood and now we had to figure out how to get it to Morro Bay. We had to find a trailer. Luckily for us, there was an old open-bed trailer for sale for reasonable money. We secured our priceless lumber and said good-bye to Helen and headed west.

In Kansas we faced a problem which actually had been predicted by a gas-station attendant. Our tires were not good enough for the load. Sure enough, we got a flat tire. Luckily, we were not far from a large truck-stop. I went in their service shop. There were some big truck drivers and I did not push my way in. Finally, I tried to put in my request with a tone of particular emergency. "I would like to have one tire, please. And see if you can look at it. I would appreciate it." I repeated it gently, but nobody responded.

Then a large fellow walked right up to the counter and with a straight, strong Kansas accent shouted, "I want some TIRES!" The word "tire" impressed me because the attendant jumped immediately and went out with him. I thought, why don't I try the same thing? I took a good breath and shouted in a similar overtone and at the same decibel as the big fellow, "I want a TIRE!" Immediately, the young attendant was right there in front of me. He went out with me and had both tires changed. We were off to California. Another drama was waiting for us, however.

It was the fourth of July, and we picked up a small American flag which was attached to our cherry tree. It looked handsome, and it made us think of George Washington. At the California border, the officer approached us slowly. I felt that he going to give us some trouble.

"What is that lumber you have on the trailer?"

"It is a cherry tree, sir, and some walnut stumps which we inherited from my relatives."

He went slowly back to the trailer and took out his writing papers. My heart started to beat faster. He came back and called another officer. He seemed to have a higher rank. I could not hear what they said, but when they started back toward the trailer with pall-bearer-like slow steps. I said in a very serious tone before they had a chance to say anything, "If you don't let us through with our inherited carving lumber, it will kill me." I don't know if it was my overtone or how I said it, but perhaps the second officer thought I was really going to do what I had said. In any case, there was a silence.

Finally, the higher ranking officer put his hand on his chin and looked at me straight in the eyes and said, "Go. You are OK." We went through the border and after a while our hearts were beating normally. We came home singing all the way to Morro Bay.

It was wonderful to watch Margaret getting used to my Georgian style of life: hiking, sculpting, traveling, cooking strange foods. It is a very organic way of living. We felt that our lives needed more than art, teaching and working. We needed family and there was one most beautiful baby waiting for us in China. We adopted our little Lia, and you should have seen Margaret's mother Inez and Lia's brother, Temmo, who were waiting at LA airport for us to greet the baby. Their faces were glowing. It was a great moment for all of us. When Lia was put in my hands by the nurse, I had a feeling which is hard to describe. I felt like a new life got inside of me, felt like I was so much younger. The same feeling I had when the newborn Temmo was put into my arms, and Tina, and finally little Ellena. Counting altogether, I became at least twenty years younger. They put so much feeling in our lives and a spark in each of us. We are the richest parents in the world, we think.

Now Temmo is 46 and Tina is 43. Lia is 14 and Ellena 9. You are wondering how old I am now. Well, I'll tell you a secret. I am 88 years old, minus 4 times 5 (one for each child) — that is 20, so I am actually 68! Thank you for your kind smile!

When Lia was three years old, we had another episode which we haven't forgotten. We received an urgent letter from my mentor, Professor Eggebrecht, my "Doktor-Vater" (doctoral 'father', or advisor) for my PhD in musicology from the University of Freiburg in Germany. He was asking us to come to Freiburg as soon as we could. It sounded urgent and having free time during the summer, we responded that we would come. The three of us flew to Germany and Dr. Eggebrecht had an apartment rented for us in a nice little village. The first evening I spent with him was a little stressful. After greetings and warm welcomes (I knew that he liked me a lot), he suddenly addressed me with a stern and serious tone. "You are the only one of my students with a PhD who has not done any post-publications, any writings or articles since your dissertation." I was stunned, quiet for a while.

Then I replied, "Yes, that is correct. I have not been writing anything, but some of us get busy teaching. Teaching, nothing but teaching. I can assure you that my writings are in my students' minds and in their hearts, and they are reading just making music alive."

He was silent. We had a glass of wine. I knew he was going to see me every evening. We said good night. I felt that he was thinking about what I said.

When we parted, he said to me, "I still want you to write."

The first week we talked about Georgian music. We agreed that the Nestorian Christianity of the early Georgians encouraged the free inter-relationship of folklore, and the strong folkloric tendency in Georgian culture had a relationship with musical expressions. The musical expression in Georgian culture became a traditional habit. There are some historical recorded impressions from 7th or 8th century BC of working songs. It was recorded that people would sing and work at the same time which gave them more energy to do more and better work. From the 4th century BC, the well-known documentation of the Greek historian Xenophon says, "The men danced and sang before fighting intruders." Another Greek geographer reports in 1st century BC such activities as horse-shoeing and wine-pressing and songs during the festivities especially during dinner times. We discussed the relationship of the folkloric lives of Georgians to their music. Heine (that was his first name — we used to call each other by first name) was getting interested and was encouraging me to write about it.

"You can still find your desk at the seminar and there is our secretary. If you need anything, she will be very happy to copy for you. You can use the library and take things with you to work on." Freiburg University was very rich in folkloric art, and I started to work every day at the seminar. The days took a very organized schedule —a typical German way. In the morning after breakfast, Margaret and Lia walked me to the railroad station. Freiburg was about half an hour by train from our little village. I worked at the library at the seminar until four o'clock every day and then went back on the train to Bad Krotzingen, that's the village where we stayed. Lia and Margaret would meet me at the station. There is something special when Daddy is arriving on the train and Mommy and the little girl run to you with welcoming open arms.

Heine and I spent every evening talking about a possible project for me. The secretary was great.

Anything I had to have, she would get and copy for me. I brought great ammunition back with me which I was going to use eventually. I had to promise Heine that I would work on the project as soon as I retired. During my teaching years, there was not enough time to devote to the project. We departed as always, in good spirits. Two years later, I received another urgent letter from the University of Freiburg, requesting me to come back. Prof. Eggebrecht passed away and they would like to have me as a pall-bearer. I was back in Germany again. We buried Heine and it was good to see all my colleagues. Just about every one of his disciples came to the event. We all knew that he showed to us an unending power of music.

During my early time studying at Freiburg University in 1972, I missed my weekend sculpting activities. Noticing that there was a stone carving institute associated with the university, I tried my luck getting into the institute. After introducing myself and explaining my intentions to the office, I was directed to see Profession Schumacher. He turned out to be very understanding and let me have a locker for my tools and aprons.

"It is fine to have you with us, but we cannot put you in a classroom situation if you are not enrolled as a student. However, you are welcome to use the outdoor covered workshop on the weekend and Friday afternoons. There are plenty of stones in the yard and you may choose any one to work on." That was welcome news!

I started going there very religiously. After some observation of the students' carving activities, I noticed that they had a very strict rule of using the point systems which involved a precision measuring from one point to the other. The goal was perfect geometric precision.

As I started to work outside in the shed and enjoyed my privacy, sometimes students from the classroom would come out and observe me. Soon I noticed the curious looks from students. I also noticed that during the recess some of them would stare from windows, point at me and chuckle. I was curious about this and asked Prof. Schumacher what was so funny.

"Oh, they told me about the strange way that you carve the stone without any point system and without using the measuring tools."

Well, that did not bother me. I went on with my way of carving. It was the way George taught me to do it. I think my pride was in the way, and I continued working on a very nice pelican sculpture. Things soon changed suddenly.

Prof. Schumacher came down himself to see how I was doing. He looked very pleased and we talked about carving technique.

"I see that you follow your feelings more than 'anatomical precision.'" I felt that he was complimenting me. "Do you mind if I bring my class and talk about your approach?"

"Of course, I'd be pleased," I replied.

The next Friday he brought his class, all sixteen of them, and started to lecture.

"When you grow out of constant measuring, you should listen to your inner feelings." He went on to talk about my pelican and the importance of expressionism. A week later he asked if I would be willing to donate the sculpture for a permanent display of students' work in the school gallery. That encouraged me to do more and I managed to have some more shows in Germany.

Later in my teaching career, I was determined to introduce and share my commitments to sculpting with my students. Since music was taken out of the school curriculum, I decided to retire from the public schools in

1984, and I approached my friend Lyle Porter, the principal of Mission College Preparatory School in San Luis Obispo. Mr. Porter was trying to hire me to his private college preparatory school to start a string-instruments program and some humanities classes.

I said, "What about adding a sculpture class? If you do this, I will definitely teach for you". He was excited about it.

"What about the studio? Where will you have the stone carving?" I had in mind the unused covered area next to the shower facilities and I suggested that we could use that area very well. It was ventilated from the sides to evacuate the dust. I was happy to see him as enthusiastic as I was.

We scheduled the classes. I requested the morning class for the string program. That was a problem with scheduling and we decided to have it one hour before the first bell. That worked out great. The humanities class was before the sculpting which was scheduled the hour before lunch. I worked out to everyone's satisfaction. I was able to be home for lunch and have my piano students in the late afternoons.

The sculpting took off in a dazzling tempo. We started to have semester shows and the attendance was very encouraging. One student, Chris Hill, who later became an accomplished sculptor, was showing impressive work. His parents were always there for the exhibits and volunteered to build a complete studio with all the necessary equipment. Things started to pick up. The studio was completed and we had a group of enthusiastic students.

The day we received the sad news of the Oklahoma City bombing in 1995 I asked my students for a moment of silence. At the end of that period, one of my sculpting students asked, "Why don't we sculpt a memorial for all the innocent people?" It was a great idea. A half-ton limestone was donated by Allan Ramage Stone Quarry in Adelaida, and we started the project. It took two months and some two dozen students to finish the sculpture of children, faces, teddy bears and fireman's helmets. The news picked up the activity and the school sent the message to the Oklahoma City mayor. The response was heart-warming. They wanted the sculpture for a Catholic church near the site of the bombing. When we received the invitation, the stone was shipped and five of our students and I were flown to back to dedicate the sculpture. It was a wonderful and unforgettable humanitarian event that will stay with all of us. *In Memoriam Innocentium.*

My youth symphony board was planning to celebrate the 50th birthday of the orchestra. The decision was to find a director of cinematography for the documentary movie of my life. The choice fell on Mr. Tom Walters who had an extensive career in filming documentaries.

When he and writer Hillary Grant approached me and outlined the project, my answer was, "Yes, I am happy to be asked and hope that my efforts for learning and teaching will inspire the students and show to them that the learning experience should be the entire life goal." I also suggested to include all my students who have done so. In particular, my very first student who became a world-celebrated conductor, Kent Nagano. Also my wish was that all the proceeds will go to scholarships for young musicians. The director Tom Walters and his filming crew turned out to be superior quality. The camera man and the sound engineers were great.

To complete the life story we had to go to Georgia. My dream was to show my children where I grew up. The fundraising started and I never realized how many friends I had. I like to mention at least some of them. Katie Stirling from Cambria was the first who graciously got the project started with a sizable donation. We managed to raise enough to go to Georgia. The cooperation from Georgian filmmakers was heart-warming. We had two sound engineers who became part of our project. There were nine of us including my family. My dream was coming true. My children Lia and Ellena were going to see Daddy's birthplace. Temmo and Tina were not able to join us this time but I plan to get them there also.

I asked Kent to join us and was disappointed that he could not do it at that time. He was familiar with Georgia. A few years before, he and I had been invited to conduct the Tbilisi Symphony Orchestra. The request was Gustav Mahler's Seventh Symphony. Kent won the hearts of not only the musicians, but all the people who heard him conduct. I was asked to do the pre-concert lecture for the Seventh Symphony, which I enjoyed very much to do, particularly in my own language.

I suggested to the film crew that we cannot complete the documentary without Kent Nagano and they all agreed. Kent became indispensible for the production. He spearheaded a successful homecoming of all my past and present students in 2008 called "Botsofest". We performed several great concerts, and it was fascinating how bonds between students, friends and all the people involved elevated the spirit, rejuvenated relationships and gave the creative energy to do more reunions. We all felt we must leave out the prefix "re-" and be united forever.

Being in Georgia for filming was the third time back for me. Again we had an enthusiastic and warm welcome. We started traveling places my dad used to introduce to me, telling me all the stories. It seemed that all the places we filmed had engravings of history. I am sure that the mental images we collected will be ours forever.

One place in particular disturbed me and threw me in a confused state. We stopped to rest in the town of Gori, the birthplace of Joseph Jugashvili — Stalin. In the middle of town, in a large court, was a nine-foot Stalin statue — the only one of its kind left in the whole former Soviet Union. After Stalin's death, Khrushchev, the new premier of the USSR, denounced Stalin and made sure that there was not any attempt to create any historical monuments, mausoleums or memorials for him.

Georgians insisted that his birthplace should be respected just for the sake of historical truth. The statue and his birthplace were left untouched.

The film crew asked me to stand by the statue for filming. I did, but I had some unusual feelings and thoughts all day. My memories came back of when I met Stalin visiting my father's theatre in Moscow. My parents' drama company, the Rustaveli Theatre, frequently did guest performances in Moscow. Since both my parents were actors, I got to go with them. At one performance which was highly acclaimed in the Soviet Union, Father told me that I should go to the performance with them instead of staying with the babysitter.

"You have a chance to see Stalin. He is scheduled to attend the play tonight."

Of course, I got excited. I could not wait for the evening. Mom made sure that I was placed in the middle of the floor level so I could look around to see Stalin.

The play started. There was not a sign of Stalin anywhere. By the last act, I fell asleep. A loud voice woke me up. I recognized the actions of the exciting third act. When I looked around, the theater was empty. I noticed four people sitting in the first row. I decided to move slowly toward the orchestra pit to see who they were. One of the KGB officers followed me silently.

I got to the front row and recognized our director Sandro Akhmeteli. Next to him was Stalin. First I was scared, but Mr. Akhmeteli was a very close friend of our family and I felt secure. I was all eyes. Next to Stalin was General Voroshilov, the head of the Soviet forces, and the last person was Mr. Sergo Ordzhonikidze, the Minister of Heavy Industry, also a Georgian.

The play came to a stage change between acts, which took about ten minutes. The four men got up to stretch and I noticed that they looked at me. I think Sandro Akhmeteli told them that I was the son of Platon Korisheli. Then it happened. Stalin singled out and moved toward me. He came and in the Georgian language asked me, "Are you proud of your father?"

I tried to swallow my saliva to be able to answer, "Yes sir, I am." He put his arm around my shoulder.

"How old are you?"

"I am twelve years."

He kept moving his hand affectionately and I think he was enjoying being able to talk in his mother language with a Georgian boy.

"Are you a good student?"

"I think I am," I answered. We were cut off by some conversations about the play, but he kept his arm around my shoulder until the bell rang for the next act. I figured out that Stalin did not come at the regular time. He came after the play was over and when the actors got the message, they restarted the whole play just for him. Well, I was accumulating some tall stories for my friends back in Georgia!

Standing next to his statue in the middle of Gori, these memories came so vividly to me that I did not know where to place them. A hundred thoughts were going through my head. I was sure he gave the okay to execute my dad and Akhmeteli two years later after our meeting. I was wrestling with my feelings. Margaret noticed my silence and disturbed facial expressions.

I decided to bury my emotions and give them to the history. Let time take care of them. I stood under the man who controlled one-fifth of the mother earth for almost half of the century with his iron hand, and I am happy that I escaped that hand.

That night I had a dream that I sculpted my father's figure as tall as Stalin's and placed him at his side with the inscription — *Usurper and Victim.*

My hope is to share all my experiences with everyone I meet. I live for the time when there will be no closed doors in the world so we can cross the threshold and shake hands and toast to unity, freedom and communication. I recall Norman Cousins, former editor-in-chief of The Saturday Review, made a trip to Georgia after the fall of the Iron Curtain. Spending two weeks there, he wrote in a piece called "Toast to Georgia" for his Saturday Review that if there should be a successful peace talk in the world, it should take place at the Georgian table.

CHAPTER NINE:

MEMORIES OF A

TEACHING LIFE

IN MUSIC

"I am still learning."

Michelangelo, after passing 70 years

T his chapter is dedicated to Professor Doktor Hans Heinrich Eggebrecht, my mentor, teacher and friend.

Dr. Eggebrecht took me under his wings and encouraged my dedication to music. I learned a wealth of scientific and natural structures of music under his guidance which enabled and enriched my teaching methods. In previous pages, I have written how Dr. Eggebrecht asked me to not only teach music but also to write about music. I shall honor his wish, and at the same time, pair my musicological report with thoughts about my teaching methods.

In my teaching career I developed two concepts for my performing students. The first is the word *scientia* (Latin), meaning learning science and knowledge that will become a mental possession. The ideal aim here is to become a master. The second: the word *eruditio* (also Latin), meaning a process of knowledge rather than possession of knowledge. This way, knowledge becomes humanity-oriented.

Both *scientia* and *eruditio* are important, but for musicians and artists, the *eruditio* should be above the *scientia*. It takes both to become an artist, for the following reasons. In our Western music we developed 88 musical sounds — notes. To use and master all of them on the keyboard, strings, or any other instrument, we have to become masters (this refers to the first concept). An artist has to go through an incredible amount of training to possess the ability to perform the music.

Then comes the second concept, the indispensable role of artistry. In music, one thing *eruditio* applies to is the ability to communicate the musical tone. *Tonsprache* (German) is the term for a "speaking tone" or "talking tone," an instrumental tone or a musical line which continues to grow and does not stop. This is a vital concept for performing musical artists.

It has been believed that a tune, or melody, or music had to have a text, a language, or words to communicate. This inseparability of text and music was particularly in practice before the 18th century. Words were thought necessary to express the emotions. But it would be wrong to assume that *Tonsprache* was never practiced before that century. Historically and psychologically we find many compositions where the music was designed to arouse the emotion and effects without the text.

Let us start with the Greeks. Pythagoras used arrangements of tetrachords to arouse the emotions.

Later, the Greeks developed their modes, which portrayed different moods (Hypodorian and Hypophrygian = tender; Hypolydian = mournful; Dorian = masterful and military; Phrygian = slack; Lydian = effeminate, soft, or convivial; Mixolydian = grieving and depressed)[1]. Putting two tetrachords together, they gained seven steps, giving the birth to our diatonic scales. We have to remember that the structure and interval relations were not like our modern scales with the home key, tonic, etc. Greeks devised the tone center so that no matter what mode the song was played in, it had to end the phrase on the tone center, called *mese*.

During the medieval times, the idea of modes and tetrachords was taken up from the ancient Greeks, although the old terminology was transferred to new modes. By the time of the Renaissance, these "new" modes were again associated with various moods. A beautiful example of tetrachords comes in the opera *Dido and Aeneas* by Henry Purcell, written at the end of the 1600s. Notice that before Dido sings her famous aria ("When I am laid in death") over many repetitions of a descending g-minor "lament tetrachord," we have a sensitively executed passage of the same tetrachord by the

---

[1] Finney, T. M. *History of Music*. rev. ed. New York: Harcourt, Brace & Co., 1949 (18-19).

lower strings announcing the final breath. After Dido's aria, the strings reinforce the mood by a breath-taking pianissimo to reinforce the effect.

The real change in the text-dominating-music idea was initiated after the end of the 17th century and beginning of the 18th century, particularly with the "Mannheim school" of orchestral writing which marked the beginning of expressivity in instrumental music. The emotional effects began to be composed into the phrases and in tone and interval relationships, even without any text. The full flower came with the time of Mozart, Beethoven, Schubert and their contemporaries.

It is unfortunate that we do not have recordings of Mozart, Beethoven or Schubert playing their own works. I am convinced that they never performed the works the same way twice. To indicate how the phrase should be correctly played, they accurately indicated in compositions to signal the effects.

Let us look at Beethoven's letter to one of the performers of his quartet Op. 132, Karl Holz, written from Baden in August 1825.

"Most excellent *Secondo Violino!*

"The passage in the 1st violin part of the first Allegro is as follows:

"Play it thus.

"Also in the first Allegro add these expression marks in the four parts:

"All the notes are all right — only understand my meaning rightly. [...]

"Now, about your copy, my good friend. *Obbligatissimo* — but the marks *p* < > and so forth have been terribly neglected and frequently, very frequently, put in the wrong place — no doubt owing to hurry. For heaven's sake please impress on Rampel [a music copyist] to write out everything exactly as it stands. Just look carefully over what I have corrected, and you will find everything that you have to say to him. Where I have put a dot over the note, there must be no dash, and vice versa! and are not the same thing. The < are often intentionally placed *after* the notes, for instance,

The slurs must stand just as they are! It is not a matter of indifference whether you play or . […]

"Mind, this comes from an authority, so pay attention. I have spent the entire morning and the whole of yesterday afternoon correcting these two movements, and am quite hoarse with swearing and stamping […]"[2]

As we see, the letter shows extreme care about proper executions of the phrases with a detailed passage to express the *Tonsprache* as he concludes, "The notes are all right, only understand my meaning rightly."

Ever since I decided to drop my ambitions to pursue the career of a concert pianist and started teaching music, my students, colleagues and friends have encouraged me to write about my teaching methods. The truth is that I do not have any dogmatic set of methods. Every student is different with various personalities which need to be understood and taken into consideration.

The great variety of students who come to me are a welcome education for me also. Some have a good sense of rhythm, some are fortunate to have perfect pitch and some are good sight-readers. I take them where they are. I also found it very helpful to play some pieces for them with different expressions to know how the music

---

[2] *A Collection of Beethoven's Letters*, by Thomas Z. Shepard and Howard Scott. The Late Quartets, p. 11.

affects them. I also like to know what kind of sports they like. If they like the same things as I do, we communicate immediately. Once I had a chess admirer. I played chess myself since I was about seven years old. That was my father's insistence and I fell in love with the game. I even built a large outdoor chess game in my home garden with hand-carved pieces. If the student mentioned chess, we were out in my garden playing or solving some game problems. That told me a lot about my newcomer and we always found a common language. I also had a few similar cases with tennis if my student was a tennis player.

Now the big question: how do we transmit and instill all the above-discussed disciplines of music? Let me start with skill and technique. We are fortunate to have an innumerable amount of etudes which are indispensable to achieve the skill of playing piano. I found that the technical etudes should be chosen to match the student's temperament. The progress will be much accelerated. I also found that Dohnanyi's essential finger exercises were extremely important. For the best motivation for students to spend the necessary time for the techniques, I designed an exercise: First, the left hand plays chords while the right hand five fingers run up and down the first five steps of the scale. Starting on C and going up chromatically, the chord will be the student's choice, but they must make sense harmonically. I must say, some interesting and daring sounds were brought back to me. Second, the right hand plays chords and the left hand five fingers do the same as in the first exercise only in reverse. This gives them freedom to choose the harmony tastefully and develops a sense of improvisation. When a student gets to a higher level of performance, he/she must get in the habit not to neglect the aspect of technique which enables them to achieve technical difficulties and have the ability to perform artistically.

Expressivity

The German expression *Tonsprache* (speaking tones) was framed and used by performers and composers. The term *Agogik* (German) or *agogic* (English) was introduced by H. Riemann in 1884 (*Musikalische Dynamik and Agogik*), describing how not to follow strict tempos but allow some deviations. The deviations from the strict tempo were left to the interpreters which enabled them to put their own feelings and emotions into the music. Here I would like to borrow a beautiful statement from a great musicologist of the 19th century who contributed so much toward the expressions in music, Eduard Hanslick.

> Composing is a work of mind upon material compatible with mind. This material is immensely

abundant and adaptable in the composer's imagination, which builds, not like the architect, out of crude, ponderous stone, but out of the aftereffects of audible tones already faded away. Being subtler and more ideal than the material of any other art, the tones readily absorb every idea of the composer. Since tonal connections, upon relationships of which musical beauty is based, are achieved not through being linked up mechanically into a series, but by spontaneous activity of the imagination, the spiritual energy and distinctiveness of each composer's imagination make their mark upon the product as character. Accordingly, as the creation of a thinking and feeling mind, a musical composition has in high degree the capability to be itself full of ideality and feeling. This ideal content we demand of every musical artwork. It is to be found only in the tone-structure itself, however, and not in any other aspect of the work. Concerning the place of ideality and feeling in a musical composition, our view is to the prevailing view as the notion of immanence is to that of transcendence.[3]

Now, how are we going to teach this type of "speaking tones"? I would like to start with one of my unforgettable cases with my dear student Colin Hannon.

Colin was almost fifteen years old when he approached me.

"I would like to learn how to play piano."

"Have you had any piano lessons before?" I asked. The answer was "no." There was such a wishful

[3] Hanslick, Eduard. *On the Musically Beautiful: A Contribution towards the Revision of the Aesthetics of Music.* Translated and Edited by Geoffrey Payzant from the Eighth Edition (1891) of *Vom Musikalisch-Schönen: ein Betrag zur Revision der Asthetik der Tonkunst.* Hackett Publishing Company. p.31

tone in his questions that I knew he was going to be a good student. He tested very well. Within a year and a half Colin acquired an impressive technique. Next it was time for the poetics – the expression.

I tried all kind of stories to express emotions and transfer the music. Nothing worked. Finally, I asked him to write a short story about something happy or sad which would excite him and excite me also. He surprised me with a very moving little story about a pet rabbit he had had. One day the rabbit disappeared. He forgot to close the cage door and the little fellow explored the neighborhood. After four days a playmate a block away saw a man catching the rabbit. When the boys knocked at the man's door, he told them, "Yes, we got lucky and caught the rabbit. Both my wife and I love rabbit goulash. It was a great dinner." My student was shocked and mourned the loss of the rabbit for some time. He wrote the story and gave it to me. I read between the lines that he was very upset. I took the opportunity and played a little sad, emotional improvisation for him. He listened intently and I could not believe the effect that lesson had on him, and I must say, on me also.

He is now an accomplished pianist and we have a close friendship. Recently he was visiting me. As usual I asked him to play for me what he was working on. He played Mozart *Fantasia* in C-minor from Sonata No. 18. That was the piece we had worked on very long ago.

"But, but…I do not remember all the nuances you are doing now," I said. His answer was beautiful.

"I know. Remember the story you made me write about my rabbit? I incorporated it into Mozart's *Fantasia.* Remember we studied Mozart during my senior year? I recently found my old writings and that story inspired me to play the *Fantasia* again, which I love so much."

That meeting was very meaningful and educational for both of us. His playing was beautiful. It made me think: what a wonderful example for all of us to be able to sing a song, recite a poem, play an instrument with our own feelings, inflections, emotions — to use *agogics.* In short, to be an artist.

I would like to bring up another good example. I had another very gifted child, Nancy Nagano. I had her on piano and later she switched to cello. She started to get an unusually beautiful, warm sound out of the instrument while she was progressing very well. I was dreaming for an orchestral sound for my Youth Symphony. A curious thing happened. I was trying to find a school for my further studies to pursue my advanced studies. I was accepted to Freiburg University in

Germany. I received a sabbatical and had to leave my young students for a year. When I got back, the first thing I inquired about was how my musicians were doing. All were all right except for Nancy. Her mother approached me and said, "You better see Nancy. She does not play the cello anymore."

I never knew that I could get so upset and furious. I stepped in and put her back on the cello again. That turned out to be a blessing for all of us. Now she is a great artist and very much in demand in the performing world. During my second sabbatical I did not take any chances. I decided to take my promising students with me. Nancy's cousin Joan Nagano was doing outstanding work on the piano. After conferring with their parents, I invited both of them to go with me to Freiburg. The Freiburg Conservatory had a great reputation and the families were agreeable with the project. Joan and Nancy both graduated with honors and now they are busy in the performing world.

The support for all my efforts would not have been as complete without the Nagano family. I had all their children and three of them became well-known. Joan Nagano started piano when she was in second grade. Her response to music was amazing. I knew that I had an accomplished musician in front of me. She was meeting all my expectations. Then her brother Kent amazed me also. I remember one remarkable thing about Kent. Once I handed out new music to sight-read. As we were rehearsing I noticed that Kent was not looking at the music anymore and was playing the right notes. Kent is now a world-renowned conductor, highly in demand in the musical world. Another great thing to come out of that family is that Nancy took over my Youth Symphony and is doing a great job. The beautiful small town of Morro Bay supported music tirelessly and the result was happy and fruitful for so many who joined my Youth Symphony. I was blessed with so many, many students and more than a dozen became professional musicians.

Theory and Ear-training

Introducing the historical development of scales is important. The students develop a wide spectrum of the evolutionary progress of scale structures and a good concept of our diatonic scales. I started introducing the tetrachord structures. (For example, our diatonic scale is made up of two tetrachords, a lower and an upper, with identical intervallic structures (whole step-whole step-half step) which are the fundaments to our melodic structures.) We can explore innumerable melodic combinations, diatonic functions, question/answer melodies, counter-melodies, interval relations, chordal structures, modulations, and more. For the students who were developing an interest in advanced theory I recommended *Mastering Music Fundamentals* by Michael Kinney (published by Thomson-Schirmer). In my teaching I also use *Melodia: A Course in Sight-Singing Solfeggio* by Samuel W. Cole and Leo R. Lewis (Oliver Ditson Co.); *Solfège des solfèges* by Danhauser, Lavignac, and Lemoine (ed. Henry Lemoine); and *Dictées musicales* by Nicole Philiba (ed. Gerard Billaudot).

For ear-training and sight-singing (solfege) I built a twelve-step staircase in my music studio to mirror the 12 chromatic tones in the scale. The studio was built with a mezzanine-balcony for acoustical reasons to interrupt the sound waves. The balcony needed a staircase to connect with the floor and that's what gave me the idea to make sure that there were twelve steps. It served two purposes: ear-training, and focusing pitch-orientation for where the students were, musically, in a composition.

The ear-training went like this: I would choose the scale and play it on the piano, but it was not visible to the student. They had to follow the sound in different directions, up and down. Sometimes I would skip a step or two, and so on. Then I would stop on some pitch and the student should know what note they were standing on. For example, I played a B-flat scale, in the process of playing I'd stop on one note, let us say the 4th step of the scale. The answer should be E-flat. Then I'd skip a major 3rd, the answer should be G, and so on.

On a chromatic scale, they should recognize the half- and whole-steps and also skips of major 3rd and minor 3rd, etc. This type of exercise not only gives them the familiarization with scales, key signatures and intervals, but also the capacity of orientation to know where they are. The training also became good for taking dictation.

I would like to describe one incident. I had a young student with a very dedicated mother who would never miss her daughter's lesson. (I always encourage parents to be part of their child's lessons.) After about half a year, the mother asked if she could try the twelve steps. I enthusiastically invited her to do so. The child became much more alert after mom's participation and she started to compete with her mom. It became the healthiest competition and the daughter was always ahead of the mother. I harvested four things from that method:

1). Parents witness and participate in lessons.

2). Parents become my assistants by making sure that the assignment was completed and students feel that the parent is part of their success.

3). Family gets musical education if they did not have exposure before.

4). And I had fun.

My twelve steps helped me also in developing a strong visual and mental imagery, a good concept of the musical spectrum.

Some of my students were able to memorize orchestral scores. I never forgot how Kent Nagano developed not just orientational powers, but also a photographic memory.

In my final statement, I would like to remind my students that the spoken language is always connected to statements, arguments, politics or asking questions, expecting answers and responses. The musical language, on the other hand, does not have arguments; it is free and always ready to be shared, always ready to become part of everyone.

Looking back at all the fortunate lives I have had, how lucky am I to be able to share it all in my writings with you, and I wish you the same kind of happiness as I have had in this world of ours. To quote my friend Paul Severtson: after reading my book he said, "You never stop. It keeps going and going." Yes, I am still going, Paul — wish me luck!

To finish, I would like to share a beautiful letter I received from my talented and dear student, Joan Nagano.

> This is a very personal message to Botso, my great teacher, counselor and friend, who sparked and fanned that first flame of musical desire when I was a young child. Today, almost thirty years later, that flame burns more brightly than ever, shedding its warmth over my life and, I hope, spilling over and felt by those who cross my path. Words cannot begin to express my appreciation for your tireless attention and concern, and the impact that the vast wealth of emotions, values and experiences you have helped me to discover has had on my life. We see each other seldom now, but our mutual past and your gifts to me are forever bonded with my personal chemistry. You are part of me. I can only hope to carry on as you have been doing for as long as I can remember: Fully embracing life, optimistically and bravely, with love, commitment, and a healthy dose of that childlike wonder and joy which this "Botso" marvelously, has never lost.
>
> With love and my deepest respect,
> your Joan

EPILOGUE

D ogs have always been part of my life. Stories about dogs were always a pleasure for me to read. I once came across an unusual and heart-warming newspaper story about a family vacationing with their dog some thousand miles away from their home in a different state. It somehow happened that the dog was left behind. They could not find their dog and came home grieving his loss. Two months later, the dog found his way home and rejoined the family.

Recently, I was asked to be a guest conductor for our high school band. It was the same school where I had brought up young musicians for more than twenty-five years. Same room, same stand where I used to do my work. I enjoyed rehearsing the concert band and was engrossed deeply in the music. After I dismissed the group, a strange thing happened to me. I wandered from the music room to the administration building, went in to the teacher's room and started toward the staff mailboxes. I stopped in front of the case where my box used to be. There were some teachers sitting in the room and when I turned around, they were staring at me. Their expressions said, "What is wrong with that man?"

Suddenly, the story of the lost dog flashed in my mind and I howled, "A-ooooo!" in a good dog imitation.

One teacher got up looking concerned. "Are you all right, sir?"

I broke out in laughter and told them the whole story. Being lost for more than thirty years, I found my place. We had a good laugh together and I picked up good new friends again.

My teaching career has been going on for over half a century. Going back in my memories, every one of my engagements in instruction has given me warm feelings and happy recollections of relationships with my students. My hope is that my life biography will encourage more key teachers like the ones I was fortunate to have. My teachers did not leave any door or window of knowledge locked to me. My wish is that every student will have the same fortune.

My father's words come back to me: "When sons and daughters do better than parents, the country will prosper."

APPENDIX:

THE STRUGGLE

OF THE CAUCASIAN

PEOPLE

FOR INDEPENDENCE

[written in 1957 for Prof. Marvin Mudrick]
[University of California, Santa Barbara]

Outline

1. Geographical location
2. History
3. The First Invasion
4. Struggle to Maintain Christianity
5. Russo-Caucasian Relation
6. Russians expansion in Caucasus
7. Restoration of Independence
8. Bolsheviks Conquest of Caucasia
9. Conclusion

Bibliography

Baddeley, J. F. *The Russian Conquest of the Caucasus*. New York, Bombay, and Calcutta: Longmans, Green and Co., 1908.

Curtis, W. E. *Around the Black Sea*. Hodder and Stoughton New York, George H. Doran Co. New York, April 15, 1912.

Essad-Bey. *Blood and Oil in the Orient*. London: Nash and Grayson. 1930.

Essad-Bey. *Twelve Secrets of the Caucasus*. New York: The Viking Press, 1931.

Gibbons, H. A. *The Blackest Page of Modern History*. New York and London: G. P. Putnam's Sons; The Knickerbocker Press, 1916.

Nansen, F. *Through the Caucasus to the Volga*. Translated by G. C. Wheeler. New York: W. W. Norton and Co., Inc., 1931.

Trotsky, L. *Stalin*. Edited and translated from the Russian by Charles Malamuth. New York and London: Harper and Brothers.

Villari, L. *Fire and Sword in the Caucasus*. London: T. Fisher Unwin Adelphi Terrace, 1906.

Caucasia lies between two continents — Europe and Asia — separated from the former by the Black Sea and from the latter by the Caspian Sea. Caucasia represents a border of each of these two continents, and is therefore a country of Eastern Europe as well as of Western Asia.

Politically, Caucasia is divided into two parts — North Caucasia and South Caucasia (or Transcaucasia). The dividing line between the two is the crest of the main chain or the watershed of the Great Caucasus range.

Caucasia has an area geographically speaking of about 380,000 sq. km. When speaking of the contemporary history of Caucasia, we have to consider separately four groups of Caucasian peoples: the North Caucasians, the Azerbaijanians, the Georgians, and the Armenians. These four countries have together a population of about 12 million.

Caucasia is one of the oldest civilized countries of the ancient world. Statements concerning Caucasia are to be found in the Old Testament and in Assyrian and Greek classics; scholars and students of the ancient cultures of mankind refer to the Caucasian tribes as having made great contributions to those civilizations. In Assyria and Greece, for instance, the discovery of

255

fabricating iron and other metals was attributed to the Caucasians, as were the selective breeding of horses and improved methods of wine-dressing.

In their political life and social order, the ancient Caucasians were equally advanced. For example, in Georgia, there were twenty-four political divisions or "kingdoms," each autonomous, but joined in a communal military alliance for the purpose of resisting outside aggression.

During the period of the Greek Argonaut raids, the western part of Georgia-Colchis was already a well-organized state with laws of its own. In the fifth century B.C., Georgia was composed of two civilized states, Colchis and Iberia, which occupied a noteworthy position in the Hellenic cultural circle.

After long wars against Persia and Rome in the first century, Georgia succeeded in entering into an agreement with the Roman Empire which assured its independent statehood. Henceforth the development of Georgian national culture proceeded unhindered within the confines of the Graeco-Roman world, and Georgia became one of the most important centers of European civilization in the Near East.

Armenia, also one of the oldest of all Christian countries in the world, was a powerful nation.

It was a powerful nation at the advent of Christ, although at different periods in its history it was occupied by the Persians under Cyrus, the Macedonians under Alexander the Great, and the Romans under the Caesars. One of the kings of Armenia, Tigranes II, made a treaty with Pompey under which he submitted to a protectorate from Rome, but after his death his son and successor, Artavasdes III, rebelled and was severely chastised by Mark Anthony, and taken prisoner to Alexandria, where he was beheaded in the year 30 B.C. by order of Cleopatra (Curtis, 150).

In the North and Western Caucasus, in the highlands and along the Black Sea coast, there are the remnants of many "autochthonous peoples, of great interest to ethnographers, who once played a large role in these lands, viz., the Circassians, to whom are allied the Kabardins, and the Abkhazians" (Villari, 23).

After the decline of Rome, Caucasia had even closer relations with the Byzantine Empire, which carried on the Hellenic-Roman tradition.

Almost simultaneously with Constantine the Great, early in the 4th century, King Mirian of Georgia declared Christianity the state religion and thereby associated his kingdom forever, spiritually and culturally, with Christian Europe.

The acceptance of Christianity made Caucasian relations with Persia more difficult and complicated and gave rise to long, intermittent warfare with that country. From the fourth century to our own times the freedom of Caucasia has been constantly endangered by reason of the nation's fidelity to Christianity.

Armenia was converted to Christianity in the year 259 A. D. by St. Gregory, "the Enlightener." The Emperor Constantine did not accept Christianity until thirty years or more afterward (Curtis, 154).

Until the thirteenth century Caucasia prospered. The eleventh to the thirteenth centuries were the golden era of Caucasian history.

It has been established that the concept of the free individual, equality of the sexes from a political aspect, and other such ideals gained headway in Georgia long before their acceptance in Western Europe. At the time of Queen Thamar (1184-1213) a reform program was set up whereby legislative and executive powers were entrusted to a kind of parliament, leaving the monarch only the rights of veto and confirmation.

Here is what Luigi Villari reports about Queen Thamar: "She does seem to have been a great woman, and to have raised her country to a high place among nations. She waged war successfully against both Turks and Greeks, and after the fall of the Byzantine Empire at the hands of crusaders, she helped to form the Empire of Tribizond" (Villari, 28).

In the thirteenth century, Caucasia suffered its first invasion by the Mongols. The country was devastated, the population was decimated, the most valuable cultural monuments were laid in ruins, and the political unity of the kingdoms was annihilated.

Caucasia would nevertheless have been able to rebuild its political, economic and spiritual life had it not suffered further Mongol invasions, ending in a domination that lasted two hundred years, until the fifteenth century. The savage Tamarlane destroyed, burned and demolished everything in order to subjugate the Caucasian race.

These Mongol depredations were the greatest catastrophe ever suffered by the Caucasian people, their political institutions and their culture. But even the Mongols were unable to wipe out Caucasia, and after their departure in the fifteenth century the people began to recover and rebuild.

From the sixteenth to the eighteenth century, Caucasia was again beset by enemies: Persia, mighty once more, and the Turkish Empire revived their old warfare for the possession of the Caucasus.

The Mongol, Persians, and Turkish attacks forced the Caucasian nations to seek assistance from the Christian sovereigns of Western Europe. Ambassadors were sent to the Pope, to the kings of France and of Spain, and later to the Holy Roman Emperor, endeavoring to bring about eventual joint action by European and Caucasian forces against the common Islamic foes. The help so sorely needed was never forthcoming from the West, and so Caucasia was urged to turn to Russia, which shared a common religion — the Greek Orthodox.

"Elizabeth dies in December 1761. Peter III succeeded and was soon murdered. From 1762 Catherine reigned alone, and the affairs of the Caucasus attracted her attention" (Baddeley, 5).

In 1783, Heraklius II, King of Georgia, concluded a protective treaty with the Russian empress. This treaty forced Georgia to accept the Russian protectorate and to agree to form no pact with any other state. In return, Russia guaranteed the absolute security of the Caucasus and military protection against all enemies. Persia protested vehemently against the treaty and demanded its immediate repudiation by the Georgian King. Heraklius refused. Thereupon, the Persian Shah Agha-Mohammed-Khan invaded Caucasia.

Russia sent no troops to aid Caucasia. Russia, however, faced with the danger of losing its influence and authority, now sent troops to Caucasia to fight against any new danger of enemy invasion.

The aid was too late. Agha-Mohammed-Khan ordered the Persian army to retire. The reason for this sudden withdrawal probably was that the Shah did not consider the war completed; in all likelihood he realized that, with his reduced army, he would be unable to withstand an attack of freshly organized Caucasia. Russia ostensibly as an ally and protector, annihilated the political freedom of an ancient civilization that had for centures been defending its national independence against countless foes; Caucasia was transformed into a Russian province.

A fighting people with the proud past of the Caucasians could not easily accept the loss of political and national freedom. From 1801 until the First World War, more than twenty-eight armed revolts took place in Caucasia. With equal energy, the North Caucasians fought against Russian domination.

For sixty years, Russia had to make war upon the Caucasian peoples before she finally succeeded in dominating them.

The Russians, having brought the war with Persia and Turkey to an end, turned again in strength against the tribes in the Caucasus, and in 1830 tried to force a way with their troops into Daghestan and Chechnia; but in the brave and daring Kasi-Mullah they found a dangerous opponent (Nansen, 129).

In 1837, during the continuous fight of the North Caucasians with Russia, an unforgettable hero (named Shamil) appeared upon the field. Here is what Mr. F. Nansen has to report about Shamil:

The Russians once more thought they had wholly broken down mountaineers' resistance. This new leader was to hold his own against mighty Russia for twenty-five years. With his comparatively few followers, he defeated the Russians time after time; and each time they thought they at last had him in their grasp, he slipped through their hands mysteriously, and attacked them soon again from another side. It was as though he was in league with supernatural powers (Nansen, 141).

At the end of the First World War, Georgia, taking advantage of the Russian revolution of 1917, re-established her political independence, thus finally rejoining the community of free peoples.

The independent life of the four Caucasian republics — Georgia, Armenia, North Caucasia and Azerbaijan — was, however, short. Soon Moscow armies invaded and occupied the provinces one by one. Thus, for the second time, in the period from 1901-1921, Russia destroyed Caucasian independence by force.

The Russian-Bolshevik reign of terror began in Caucasus immediately after the conquest of 1921. Members of the government and of the legislative body and a great many of the intelligentsia left Caucasia and took up residence in Western Europe. While the Bolsheviks have apparently accorded political autonomy to the oppressed countries and taken them into the Soviet Union as "free states," in reality their entire life is dependent on Moscow; while proclaiming the advantages of socialist production methods, the Bolsheviks plunder the people economically, and by abrogation of private ownership, they ruined the national economy, particularly the farming, through the "Kolkoz" or collective farm.

The population is forced to adapt the entire economic system to the needs of Moscow's eternal war aims.

As already mentioned above, as soon as the Russian Revolution broke out in 1917, Georgia immediately profited by the occasion. On May 26, 1918, the independence of the Republic of Georgia was proclaimed.

During the next three years, Georgia proved to the world that she was able again to manage her own affairs. More than twenty nations, including Great Britain, France, Italy, Belgium, and Japan, extended their recognition to the young republic. A treaty of friendship and alliance was signed between Georgia and the Soviet Union again. However, only eight months later, in February 1921, without declaration of war, the Red Army attacked Georgia and, after several months of a bitter, unequal fight, occupied the country.

Several attempts by the Bolsheviks to seize power during the period of Georgian independence were easily suppressed due to the energy of the national government and the militantly independent attitude of the people.

Only a small number of Georgian revolutionaries adopted the Bolshevik teachings. Among them were Joseph Jugashvili (Stalin), Orjonikidse, Beria, et al. Not having any advance among the Georgian people, who were highly inspired by freedom and independence, the active Georgian Bolsheviks went to Russia. There they joined their chief, Jugashvili, and organized the Russian attack on their own land, leading the Russian troops into Caucasia.

After Georgia had been overrun and occupied by foreign troops, a small number of local communists undertook to persuade the world that a spontaneous internal change of regime had taken place in Georgia and that the Red Army occupied the country with a view to "helping and protecting the Georgian proletariat against capitalist oppressors" (no citation). This was done according to Lenin's instructions.

All these events prove that the independence of Georgia has been smothered and annihilated by the intervention of foreign troops.

Another proof of this fact can be found in the writings of Trotsky (Commissar of the War Ministry of the Russian Soviet Republic at that time); in his book "Stalin," published in exile, he made the following remarks: "The Georgian people, almost entirely peasant or petty bourgeois in composition, resisted vigorously the sovietization of their country" (Trotsky, no page given).

As Stalin marched into Caucasian regions, Trotsky wrote, "It looks as if Stalin had forgotten that we had signed on May 7, 1920, a pact of friendship and non-aggression with Georgia and then on February 11, 1921, the Red Army, upon his order, crossed the Georgian border" (Trotsky, 358). Trotsky at that time was trying to put all the blame on Stalin and shift the responsibility over to him. But it should be kept in mind that if their personal relations had remained friendly and the final split had not occurred, putting Trotsky to the necessity of leaving the country and going into exile, the question of the occupation of Georgia by the Red Army would have been different altogether. The plan to annex all Caucasian nations was inevitable as we know.